||||| ||| |||||| || ||| |||||||||||||||||| ||| |||

⊲ **W9-DDN-123**

THE METAMORPHOSIS AND OTHER STORIES

WITHDRAWN NOTES

including
- *Life and Background*
- *Commentaries on the Stories*
- *Understanding Kafka*
- *Kafka's Jewish Influence*
- *Kafka—a "Religious" Writer?*
- *Kafka and Existentialism*
- *Review Questions*
- *Selected Bibliography*

by
Herberth Czermak, M.A.
Instructor
Amerika Institut, Vienna

Cliffs® Notes
INCORPORATED

LINCOLN, NEBRASKA   68501

Editor

Gary Carey, M.A.
University of Colorado

Consulting Editor

James L. Roberts, Ph.D.
Department of English
University of Nebraska

ISBN 0-8220-0700-2
© Copyright 1973
by
C. K. Hillegass
All Rights Reserved
Printed in U.S.A.

1993 Printing

Cliffs Notes, Inc.   Lincoln, Nebraska

CONTENTS

Kafka's Stories Notes

LIFE AND BACKGROUND

Born in Prague in 1883, Franz Kafka is today considered the most important prose writer of the so-called Prague Circle, a loosely knit group of German-Jewish writers who contributed to the culturally fertile soil of Prague during the 1880s until after World War I. Yet from the Czech point of view, Kafka was German, and from the German point of view he was, above all, Jewish. In short, Kafka shared the fate of much of Western Jewry—people who were largely emancipated from their specifically Jewish ways and yet not fully assimilated into the culture of the countries where they lived. Although Kafka became extremely interested in Jewish culture after meeting a troupe of Yiddish actors in 1911, and although he began to study Hebrew shortly after that, it was not until late in his life that he became deeply interested in his heritage. His close relationship with Dora Dymant, his steady and understanding companion of his last years, contributed considerably toward this development. But even if Kafka had not been Jewish, it is hard to see how his artistic and religious sensitivity could have remained untouched by the ancient Jewish traditions of Prague which reached back to the city's tenth-century origin.

In addition to Kafka's German, Czech, and Jewish heritages, there was also the Austrian element into which Kafka had been born and in which he had been brought up. Prague was the major second capital of the Austrian Empire (after Vienna) since the early sixteenth century, and although Kafka was no friend of Austrian politics, it is important to emphasize this Austrian component of life in Prague because Kafka has too often been called a Czech writer—especially in America. Kafka's name is also grouped too often with German writers, which is accurate only in the sense that he belongs to the German-speaking world. Apart from that, however, it is about as meaningful as considering Faulkner an English novelist.

For his recurring theme of human alienation, Kafka is deeply indebted to Prague and his situation there as a social outcast, a victim of the friction between Czechs and Germans, Jews and non-Jews. To understand Kafka, it is important to realize that in Prague the atmosphere of medieval mysticism and Jewish orthodoxy lingered until after World War II, when the Communist regime began getting rid of most of its remnants. To this day, however, Kafka's tiny flat in Alchemists' Lane behind the towering Hradschin Castle is a major attraction for those in search of traces of Kafka. The haunting mood of Prague's narrow, cobble-stoned streets, its slanted roofs, and its myriad backyards comes alive in the surreal settings of Kafka's stories. His simple, sober, and yet dense language is traced to the fact that in Prague the German language had been exposed to manifold Slavic influences for centuries and was virtually cut off from the mainstream language as spoken and written in Germany and Austria. Prague was a linguistic island as far as German was concerned, and while the Czech population of Prague doubled within the last two decades of the nineteenth century, the percentage of German Jews sank to a mere seven percent. The result was that Kafka actually wrote in a language which was on the verge of developing its own characteristics. This absence of any gap between the spoken and written word in his language is probably the secret behind the enormous appeal of his language, whose deceptive simplicity comes across in every decent translation.

Kafka's family situation was a reflection of his being a German-speaking Jew in a predominantly Slavic environment. The great socio-economic and educational differences between his father, Hermann Kafka, and his mother, Julie Löwy, were at the root of this complex situation. Kafka's father's whole life was shaped by his desperate and eventually successful attempt to break out of his poor Czech milieu and become accepted in the prestigious environment of German Prague; his mother, however, came from a wealthy German-Jewish bourgeois family. Throughout his lifetime, Franz Kafka could never extricate himself from the terrible friction between his parents which was caused, for the most part, by his tyrannical father. Kafka's only strong, positive ties with his family were with his favorite sister,

Ottla, who let him stay at her home and later helped him break off his relationship with Felice, his first fiancée. To one extent or another, all of Kafka's works bear the unmistakable imprint of the nerve-wracking struggle between his humility and hypersensitivity (his mother's heritage) and the crudity and superficiality of his father, who looked at his son's writing with indifference and, at times, with contempt. This total lack of understanding and the absence of any home life worthy the name (young Franz was virtually brought up by a nurse) caused the boy's early seriousness and anxiety. As late as 1919, five years before his death, this lifelong trauma manifested itself in his *Letter to His Father* (almost a hundred pages, but never actually delivered), in which Kafka passionately accuses his father of intimidation and brutality. Although it will not do to reduce the complex art of Franz Kafka to its autobiographical elements, the significance of these elements in his work is indeed striking. His story "The Judgment" seems especially to be the direct result of his deep-seated fear of his father.

Kafka is the classical painter of the estrangement of modern man, although he is never its apostle. As early as 1905, in his "Description of a Fight," Kafka already denied man's ability to obtain certainty through sensory perception and intellectual effort because, according to him, these methods inevitably distort the nature of the Absolute by forcing it into their prefabricated structures. The resulting skepticism, of which he himself was to become the tragic victim, was the basis of his conviction that none of our fleeting impressions and accidental associations have a fixed counterpart in a "real" and stable world. There is no clear-cut boundary between reality and the realm of dreams, and if one of his characters appears to have found such a boundary, it quickly turns out that he has set it up merely as something to cling to in the face of chaos. The "real" world of phenomena develops its own logic and leaves Kafka's characters yearning for a firm metaphysical anchor which they never quite grasp.

At no time did Kafka seek refuge from his culturally and socially alienated situation by joining literary or social circles — something many of his fellow writers did. He remained an outcast, suffering from the consequences of his partly self-imposed seclusion, and yet welcoming it for the sake of literary productivity. Anxious although he was to use his positions, as well as his engagements to Felice Bauer and Julie Wohryzek, as a means to gain recognition for his writing, his life story is, nevertheless, one long struggle against his feelings of guilt and inferiority.

The one person who could and did help him was Max Brod, whom he met in 1902 and who was to become not only his editor but also an intimate friend. The numerous letters which Kafka wrote to him are a moving testimony of their mutual appreciation. Because of Brod's encouragement, Kafka began to read his first literary efforts to small private audiences long before he was recognized as a significant writer. With Brod, Kafka traveled to Italy, Weimar (where Goethe and Schiller had written), and Paris; later, Brod introduced him into the literary circles of Prague. In short, Brod helped Kafka to fend off an increasingly threatening self-isolation. Most significantly for posterity, it was Brod who, contrary to Kafka's express request, did not burn the manuscripts which Kafka left behind; instead, he became their enthusiastic editor.

If Kafka had a strong inclination to isolate himself, this does not mean he was indifferent to what was going on around him. Especially in the years until 1912, Kafka familiarized himself with some of the far-reaching new ideas of the day. At a friend's house, he attended lectures and discussions on Einstein's theory of relativity, Planck's quantum theory, and Freud's psychoanalytical experiments. He was also interested in politics, especially the nationalistic aspirations of the Czechs in the Austrian Empire. In his function as a lawyer at the Workers' Insurance Company, he was confronted daily with the social situation of workers, and toward the end of World War I, he even composed a brochure on the plight of the proletariat. This is, in part, proof that Franz Kafka was not the melancholy dreamer of nightmares, isolated in his ivory tower in Prague—a view still commonly held today.

It was at Max Brod's home that Kafka met Felice Bauer in 1912. This encounter plunged him into a frustrating relationship for many years, oscillating between engagements and periods of complete withdrawal. "The Judgment" (1912) is a document of this encounter. Having literally poured it out in one long sitting, Kafka came to regard it as an illustration of how one should always write; it was the subject of his first public reading. At that time, Kafka was already filling a detailed diary, full of reflections and parables as a means of self-analysis. The same year, 1912, he wrote "The Metamorphosis," one of the most haunting treatments of human alienation, and most of the fragmentary novel *Amerika*. According to his own conviction, his literary productivity reached a peak at precisely the time when his insecurity and anxiety over whether or not to marry Felice reached a climax. For the first time, the deep-seated conflict between his yearning for the simple life of a married man and his determination not to succumb to it became critical.

More and more, Kafka's writing began to deal with *Angst* (anxiety, anguish), probably because of the sustained anxiety induced by his domineering father and by the problem of whether or not to break away from his bachelorhood existence. Toward the end of "The Judgment," and in "In the Penal Colony," as well as in *The Trial* and *The Castle*, the father figure assumes the mysterious qualities of an ineffable god. Suffering, punishment, judgment, trial—all these are manifestations of Kafka's rigorous, ethical mind. The philosophy of Franz Brentano, to which he was exposed at the university, intensified his interest in these themes. The essence of this philosophy is that since emotions and concepts cannot sufficiently explain moral action, personal judgment alone must determine it; thorough self-analysis is the only prerequisite for such a total autonomy of personal judgment, a view which Kafka came to exercise almost to the point of self-destruction.

Kafka's fascination with these themes received new impetus when he began to read the Danish philosopher Sören Kierkegaard in 1913. As radical a skeptic as Kafka and equally religious by temperament, Kierkegaard envisages man as caught in the dilemma of wanting to comprehend Divinity with the altogether inadequate tools of rationality. Since God's transcendence is absolute for him, Kierkegaard sees no way of solving this dilemma except by abandoning intellectual pursuit and venturing a "leap into faith." Kafka's plea for man to "enter into the law," stated most explicitly in the parable "Before the Law" (in *The Trial*), deals with this dilemma. The difference is that Kierkegaard is cornered by the overwhelming presence of God forcing him to make decisions. In Kafka's parable, his hero wants to enter the first gate of the palace—that is, "the law"—but he dies because he does not exert sufficient will to enter and leaves all possible decisions to the gatekeeper; Kafka's searching man has no divine guidance to show him the way, and the situation he faces is one of total uncertainty and despair. Antithetically, Kierkegaard's radical skepticism results in faith.

Kafka and Kierkegaard have been called existentialists, and though this label has some merits, it should nevertheless be used very carefully. Both men were fascinated by the theme of moral integrity in the face of freedom of choice and were convinced that man lives meaningfully only to the extent which he realizes himself. In this connection, it is interesting to know that Kafka felt close to Kierkegaard because of the latter's lifelong unresolved relationship to his fiancée. The problem dominated Kierkegaard's life and work as much as Kafka's life and work was dominated by his relationships with Felice Bauer (to whom he was engaged twice—in 1914 and 1917), Julie Wohryzek (engaged in 1919), and Milena Jesenska (1920-22).

Perhaps more than any other story, Kafka's "In the Penal Colony" (1914) reflects his reaction to the outbreak of World War I, a feeling of sheer horror as well as disgust with the politicians in power. The result was a renewed fascination with Schopenhauer and Dostoevsky, whose extolment of physical pain finds expression in a variety of ways. Near this same time, Kafka began working on *The Trial*, about which he remarked that its ghastly thoughts devoured him in much the same way as did his thoughts about Felice. The novel is an elaborate and heavily autobiographical fantasy of punishment: on the eve of his thirty-first birthday, Joseph K. is executed; on the evening of his own thirty-first birthday, Kafka decided to travel to Berlin to break off his first engagement with Felice. Symptomatically for Kafka, this novel remained fragmentary — as did his other two, *Amerika* and *The Castle.* "A Report to an Academy" and the fragmentary "The Hunter Gracchus" followed, and in 1919 several stories were published under the title *A Country Doctor.* The title story is a symbolic description of modern man living outside a binding universal order and brought to death by sensuality and the aimlessness of the forces working within him. This volume contains perhaps Kafka's best parable on the nature of absurdity, "The Imperial Message." It is a terrifying description of how important messages, ordered at the top level to save men at the bottom, never stand a chance of getting through the manifold obstacles of bureaucracy. "The Imperial Message" is an interesting reversal of "Before the Law," where the lowly searcher never even gets beyond the first gate (the lowest obstacle) in his attempt to proceed to higher insights. In both cases, the human need to communicate is frustrated, and the inevitable result is alienation and subsequent death.

These stories were written during a time when Kafka, engaged once again to Felice, was finding a measure of stability again. Although he was determined this time to give up his insurance position and to use his time writing, he soon realized that this effort was an escape, as had been his (rejected) application to be drafted into the army. Kafka was to remain much like the roving hunter Gracchus, burdened with the knowledge that he could not gain inner poise by drowning the fundamental questions of existence in the comforts of married life.

In 1917 Kafka was stricken with tuberculosis, an illness which he was convinced was only the physical manifestation of his disturbed inner condition. For years he had fought hopeless battles for and against marriage (he had a son with Grete Bloch, a friend of Felice's, but never knew about him); during this time, he continually sought to justify his suffering by writing. Now he gave up. "The world — Felice is its representative — and my innermost self have torn apart my body in unresolvable opposition," he wrote in his diary. His suffering was alleviated by the fact that he could spend many months in the country, either in sanatoriums or with his favorite sister, Ottla. These months brought with them a new freedom from his work as a lawyer and, for the second time, from Felice.

In 1922, Kafka wrote "A Hunger Artist," "Investigations of a Dog," and most of his third novel, *The Castle*. Highly auto-biographical like all of his works, the hero of "A Hunger Artist" starves himself because he cannot find the spiritual food he requires. The investigations of the chief dog in the story of the same name reflect Kafka's own literary attempts to impart at least a notion of the universal to his readers. In *The Castle*, K. becomes entangled in the snares of a castle's "celestial" hierarchy as hopelessly as does Joseph K. in the "terrestrial" bureaucracy of *The Trial*. All these stories originated in the years 1921 and 1922, years when Kafka lived under the strong influence of Milena Jesenska, to whom he owed his renewed strength to write. Although in many respects different from him (she was gentile, unhappily married, and much younger), the extremely sensitive Milena could justly claim "to have known his anxiety before having known Kafka himself," as she put it. Forever afraid of any deeper involvement with Milena, Kafka eventually stopped seeing her. That he gave her his diaries and several manuscripts, however, is proof of his deep commitment to her.

COMMENTARIES

"THE METAMORPHOSIS"
(DIE VERWANDLUNG)

Kafka wrote "The Metamorphosis" at the end of 1912, soon after he finished "The Judgment," and it is worth noting that the two stories have much in common: a businessman and bachelor like Georg Bendemann of "The Judgment," Gregor Samsa is confronted with an absurd fate in the form of a "gigantic insect," while Georg is confronted by absurdity in the person of is father. Also both men are guilty: like Georg in "The Judgment," Gregor Samsa (note the similarity of first names) is guilty of having cut himself off from his true self—long before his actual metamorphosis—and, to the extent he has done so, he is excluded from his family. His situation of intensifying anxiety, already an unalterable fact at his awakening, corresponds to Georg's after his sentence. More so than Georg, however, who comes to accept his judgment, out of proportion though it may be, Gregor is a puzzled victim brought before the Absolute—here in the form of the chief clerk—which forever recedes into the background. This element of receding, an important theme in Kafka's works, intensifies the gap between the hero and the unknown source of his condemnation. Thus the reader finds himself confronted with Gregor's horrible fate and is left in doubt about the source of Gregor's doom and the existence of enough personal guilt to warrant such a harsh verdict. The selection of an ordinary individual as victim heightens the impact of the absurd. Gregor is not an enchanted prince in a fairy tale, yearning for deliverance from his animal state; instead, he is a rather average salesman who awakens and finds himself transformed into an insect.

In a sense, Gregor is the archetype of many of Kafka's male characters: he is a man reluctant to act, fearful of possible mishaps, rather prone to exaggerated contemplation, and given to juvenile, surrogate dealings with sex. For example, he uses his whole body to anxiously guard the magazine clipping of a lady in a fur cape; this is a good illustration of his pitiful preoccupation with sex. Though it would be unfair to blame him for procrastinating, for not getting out of bed on the first morning of his metamorphosis, we have every reason to assume that he has procrastinated long before this—especially in regard to a decision about his unbearable situation at work. Gregor has also put off sending his sister to the conservatory, although he promised to do so. He craves love and understanding, but his prolonged inactivity gradually leads him to feel ever more indifferent about everything. It is through all his failures to act, then, rather than from specific irresponsible actions he commits, that Gregor is guilty. The price his guilt exacts is that of agonizing loneliness.

Plays on words and obvious similarities of names point to the story's highly autobiographical character. The arrangement of the vowels in *Samsa* is the same as in *Kafka*. More significantly yet, *samsja* means "being alone" in Czech. (In this connection it is noteworthy that in "Wedding Preparations in the Country," an earlier use of the metamorphosis motif, the hero's name is *Raban*. The same arrangement of the vowel *a* prevails, and there is also another play on words: *Rabe* is German for *raven*, the Czech word for which is *kavka*; the raven, by the way, was the business emblem of Kafka's father.)

It is easy to view Gregor as an autobiographical study of Kafka himself. Gregor's father, his mother, and his sister also have their parallels with Kafka's family. Gregor feels that he has to appease his father, who "approaches with a grim face" toward him, and it is his father's bombardment with apples that causes his death. The two women, on the other hand, have the best of intentions — his mother pleading for her son's life, believing that Gregor's state is only some sort of temporary sickness; she even wants to leave the furniture in his room the way it is "so that when he comes back to us he will find everything as it was and will be able to forget what has happened all the more easily." And Grete, so eager to understand and help her brother at first, soon changes; she does not want to forgo her "normal" life and is the first one to demand the insect's removal. These people simply do not understand, and the reason they do not understand is that they are habitually too "preoccupied with their immediate troubles."

Gregor's situation in his family is that of Kafka within his own family: he had a tyrannical father who hated or, at best, ignored his son's writing; a well-meaning mother, who was not strong enough to cope with her husband's brutality; and a sister, Ottla, whom Kafka felt very close to. Shortly after completing "The Metamorphosis," Kafka wrote in his diary: "I am living with my family, the dearest people, and yet I am more estranged from them than from a stranger."

Returning to the subject of Gregor, what strikes one most immediately is the fact that although he is outwardly equipped with all the features of an insect, he reacts like a human being. Gregor never identifies himself with an insect. It is important to realize, therefore, that Gregor's metamorphosis actually takes place in his "uneasy dreams," which is something altogether different than saying it is the result of the lingering impact of these dreams. An interpretation often advanced categorizes Gregor's metamorphosis as an attempt at escaping his deep-seated conflict between his true self and the untenable situation at the company. He begs the chief clerk for precisely that situation which has caused him to be so unhappy; he implores him to help him maintain his position and, while doing so, completely forgets that he is a grotesquerie standing in front of the chief clerk.

What bothers Gregor most about his situation at the company is that there is no human dimension in what he is doing: "All the casual acquaintances never become intimate friends." If it were not for his parents' debt to his chief, whom — typical of Kafka's predilection for the anonymity of top echelons — we never hear about in concrete terms, Gregor would have quit working long ago. As will be shown later, he would have had every reason to do so. As it turns out, he was, and still is, too weak. Even now in his helpless condition, he continues to think of his life as a salesman in "normal" terms; he plans the day ahead as if he could start it like every other day, and he is upset only because of his clumsiness.

Although one might expect such a horrible fate to cause a maximum of intellectual and emotional disturbance in a human being — and Gregor remains one inwardly until his death — he stays surprisingly calm. His father shows the same incongruous behavior when confronted with Gregor's fate; he acts as if this fate were something to be expected from his son. The maid treats him like a curious pet, and the three lodgers are amused, rather than appalled, by the sight of the insect. The reason for the astounding behavior of all these people is found in their incapacity to comprehend disaster. This incapacity, in turn, is a concomitant symptom of their limitless indifference toward everything happening to Gregor. Because they have maintained a higher degree of sensitivity, the women in Gregor's family respond differently at first, Gregor's mother even resorting to a fainting spell to escape having to identify the insect with her son.

Gregor's unbelievably stayed reaction to his horrible fate shows Kafka, the master painter of the grotesque, at his best. In paragraphs bristling with the most meticulous descriptions of the absurd, Kafka achieves the utmost in gallows humor and irony. Gregor's crawling up and down the wall, his delighting in dirt, and the fact that he "takes food only as a pastime" — all these are described in detail and presented as normal; at the same time, however, on the morning of his metamorphosis, Gregor "catches at some kind of irrational hope" that nobody will open the door. The comical effect of this reversal of the normal and the irrational is then further heightened by the servant girl's opening the door as usual.

Let us return to Gregor's conflict. His professional and social considerations are stronger than his desire to quit working for his company. In fact, he even toys with the idea of sleeping and forgetting "all this nonsense." This "nonsense" refers to his transformation, which he does not want to accept because he sees it only as something interfering with his daily routine. His insect appearance must not be real because it does not suit Gregor the businessman. By ignoring or negating his state, he can, of course, in no way eliminate it. The contrary seems to be the case: the more he wants to ignore it, the more horrible its features become; finally he has to shut his eyes "to keep from seeing his struggling legs."

As a representative of the run-of-the-mill mentality of modern man, Gregor is frustrated by his totally commercialized existence and yet does nothing about it, other than try to escape by new calculations along purely commercial lines. He vows that once he has sufficient money, he will quit, and yet he has no idea what he will do. He does not really know his innermost self, which is surrounded by an abyss of emptiness. This is why Kafka draws this "innermost self" as something strange and threatening to Gregor's commercialized existence.

The insect is Gregor's "innermost self." It refuses to be further subjected to the miserable life Gregor has led in his concern for money. At last it has intruded into Gregor's life and it is not going to be chased away like a ghost. Having emerged under the cover of night, as also happens in "A Country Doctor," this "self" seeks a confrontation with the other parts of Gregor Samsa. Time and time again, Kafka pictures the alienated "inner self" of his heroes in the form of animals—for instance, in "Investigations of a Dog," "The Burrow," and "A Report to an Academy." Sometimes, too, Kafka uses absurd authorities of law to represent man's suppressed and estranged "self," as in *The Trial*. In this connection, it is valuable to compare the opening scenes of this novel and our story: Joseph K. was taken by surprise immediately on awakening, just as Gregor is here. Both men were seized in the morning, during the short period of consciousness between sleep and the beginning of one's daily routine. Joseph, too, did not hear the alarm, and he, like Gregor, was taken prisoner. Both men try to shake off their fate by acting as if it did not really exist, but, in both instances, the apparent delusion turns out to be terrifying reality.

The insect represents all the dimensions of Gregor's existence which elude description because they transcend rational and empirical categories. This is why Kafka was so adamant about not having the insect reproduced in any conventional manner when the story was published. He wrote his publisher that it would be wrong to draw the likeness of the insect on the book cover because any literal representation would be meaningless. Gregor—after his metamorphosis—can be depicted only to the extent he can see and grasp himself—hence not at all or merely by implication. Here, as in *The Trial*, the world is commensurate with the hero's concept of it. The agreement which Kafka and his publisher finally reached permitted illustrating the scene at the beginning of the third part where Gregor, "lying in the darkness of his room, invisible to his family, could see them all at the lamp-lit table and listen to their talk" through the living room door.

It has been said that the story draws its title not from Gregor's metamorphosis, which is already an established fact at the beginning, but from the change which the members of his family—especially Grete—undergo as his fate fulfills itself. Indeed, in contrast to Gregor's deterioration and ultimate death, Grete's fortunes and those of her family are steadily improving. In fact, it is through her eventually negative reaction to Gregor's misfortune that Grete finds a degree of self-assurance. Her father, also as a result of Gregor's incapacitating transformation, becomes active once more and seemingly younger after years of letting his son take care of the family.

Of all the members of the family, Grete plays perhaps the most significant role in Gregor's life because with her "alone had he remained intimate." He sleeps with his face toward her room, he once promised to send her to the conservatory, and he suffers more from the emotional wounds she inflicts upon him than from the apples which his father throws at him—fatal and symbolic bullets of perniciousness though they are. There is some evidence that his relationship with Grete has strong incestual overtones, as will be shown later. This aspect of the story is also highly autobiographical. Such lines as "he would never let her out of his room, at least not as long as he lived" and "he would then raise himself to her shoulder and kiss her on the neck" certainly appear in this light. Interestingly enough, Kafka wrote in his diary in 1912 that "the love between brother and sister is but a re-enactment of the love between father and mother." Be this as it may, as soon as Grete turns against Gregor, he deteriorates rapidly. Once she convinces her family that they must get rid of the "idea that this is Gregor," they ignore him completely and eventually consult about disposing of *it*, not *him.*

The most terrible insight which the story conveys is that even the most beautiful relationships between individuals are based on delusions. No one knows what he or anybody else really is: Gregor's parents, for instance, have no idea of their son's serious conflict, much less of the extent of his sacrifice for them. As Kafka puts it, "His parents did not understand this so well." They have no idea that one's nature can be deformed by the continued degradation it suffers, but now that this deformation has taken on such horrible proportions they are puzzled and look at Gregor as something alien. Typically enough, "the words he uttered were no longer understandable." The concern they should have shown for him finds a perverted outlet in their pre-occupation with total strangers, the three lodgers who get an enormous amount of attention simply because of the rent they pay. Finally, it is only consistent with their way of thinking that Gregor's parents should do away with the insect: pretense alone makes the world go round. Put differently, truth and life are mutually exclusive.

Gregor, for example, is mistaken about his family. He has believed it was his duty to help them pay their debts and secure a financially carefree life, and he has done this by selling his soul to the company. The truth is that his father has far more money than Gregor knows about; also, he was not nearly as sick as he has made Gregor believe. Gregor's self-chosen sacrifice has been senseless. Worse than that, the more he has done for his family, the more "they had simply got used to it." Gregor's relationship with the members of his family, and also their deal-ings among each other, are determined solely by the contrived order they have set up for themselves. Their lives are based on ever-new compromises and calculations. In Gregor's "uneasy dreams," the compromises and calculations finally rupture and, from them, truth rises in the form of a "gigantic insect."

As the maid sweeps out the dead insect, the Samsas have arrived at the threshold of what looks like a bright future. The harmony between them seems to be the result of their common fate of being drawn together by the misfortune that befell them. This return of the family to a life unfettered by a tragedy like Gregor's has often been seen as proof of their hypocrisy, possibly foreshadowing the emergence of another "inner insect" from one of them. The danger of this view is that it tends to see Gregor's transformation only as a sort of psychological mech-anism, thus detracting from its uniqueness and absurdity. The basic question here is this: who is to call another person — in this case, the entire Samsa family — hypocritical simply because this other person has the strength (and perhaps brutality) necessary to overcome tragedy? Certainly not Kafka (See "A Hunger Artist").

It has been argued that the epilogue is poor because it stands as a cheerful counterpoint to the tragic and absurd metamorphosis of Gregor. No matter how natural and, therefore, justifiable the family's return to a "normal life" may be, so runs the argument, it cannot possibly make up for the horror of what has happened. We must ask ourselves, therefore, if Kafka intended this. Is it not exactly the naturalness of the family's reaction and their callousness accompanying this "healthy reaction" that emphasizes the absurdity of Gregor's fate?

The questions pertaining to Gregor's identity are central to the story. The narrator brings up this problem of identity when he asks: "Was he an animal, that music had such an effect upon him?" Since only humans respond to music in the way the insect responds to Grete's playing the violin, we realize that he is indeed part human. The violin playing is also a part of the countless allusions to Gregor's repressed sexual desires, particularly his longing for his sister. As Gregor lies in front of Grete and listens to her music, he has only her on his mind. The confusion of violin playing and player—and his inability to admit this to himself—are they part of Gregor's guilt? Did he originally want to send her to a conservatory as a kind of "messenger" to a spiritual realm? Does it mean that he, too, once wanted to become a musician? His utter loneliness illustrates the abyss into which all these questions lead. It is most clear that Gregor responds to the music only now that he is not the traveling salesman he used to be, even though he is, in part, an insect. Thus Gregor's "animal state" seems to be a precondition of his yearning for this "unknown food." This food may very well be physical—that is, sexual. The ambiguity about the nature of the food remains—as does the uncertainty about whether Gregor is experiencing only a relapse into the sphere of the animalistic or whether or not he has been lifted up to a higher plane. His identity cannot be established from his reactions because whenever Gregor is impaired as a human being, he reacts positively as an animal and vice versa. When the women in his family clean out his room, for instance, he resents this as a human being, not as an insect. By the same token, mention of his horrible appearance bothers the human element in him, whereas it is the animal in him that is hurt when he is ignored. The most plausible answer is that, although he is an insect, Gregor nevertheless transcends his animal condition, craving spiritual *and* sexual food. During his existence as a salesman, he certainly lacked both these aspects of life. ("A Hunger Artist" is the most haunting treatment of this theme of the spiritual nourishment which cannot be found on earth. Also, in "Investigations of a Dog," the central issue concerns making spiritual food available through music.) Man or animal: maybe the answer cannot be answered here or in any of Kafka's works. Despite their different interpretations, all of Kafka's animals — the insect here, as well as the horses in "A Country Doctor," and the ape in "A Report to an Academy" — have one thing in common: like Kafka's human beings, they have lost the place which divine creation originally assigned to them. Like all creatures, man or animal, Gregor has lost his identity without, however, becoming a true insect. Perhaps Gregor is best identified as belonging to the vast realm of the in-between. *His* (or *its*) agonizing anxiety reflects *his* (or *its*) fate of belonging nowhere.

As an insect, Gregor cannot communicate with his family, but he does try "to return to the human circle." Through Grete's music, he seems to accomplish this to an extent which permits him to die at peace with himself, "thinking of his family with tenderness and love." The pretense is at an end when he finally takes his spiritual (and sexual) component into account and does justice to it (them) by permitting himself to become attuned to Grete's playing (and to Grete herself).

Concerning the story's formal aspects, a few observations should be made. It is divided into three parts, each dealing with a different aspect of Gregor's attempt to break out of his imprisonment. The first one deals with his professional conflict, the second deals primarily with his reaction to the increasingly tense alienation within his family, and the last deals with Gregor's death or, expressed positively, his liberation. Throughout the story, Gregor's deteriorating condition is in direct contrast to his family's slow but steady metamorphosis from sheer horror to self-satisfaction. In a sense, the three parts correspond to the dramatic pattern of exposition, conflict, and denouement.

Within the story's three-part construction, Kafka also deals with the concept of time. Awakening from his "uneasy dreams," Gregor is fully conscious throughout the first part—that is, for one hour, beginning at half past six. His consciousness sets in too late, however, for his train left at five. A frequently used device in Kafka's works, the discrepancy between the time shown on the clock and the time as experienced by the hero symbolizes his alienation. This is why Gregor's sense of time begins to vanish in the second part, when he wakes up "out of a deep sleep, more like a swoon than a sleep." Typically, time is expressed in rather general terms, such as "twilight" or "long evening." There is no longer the regular routine of the first day; Gregor spends his time crawling up and down and around his room. Vague indications of time are reflected in such terms as "soon," "later," and "often," blurring the boundary lines between what used to be precisely measurable units of time. At one point in the story, the narrator tells us that "about a month" probably has elapsed; on another occasion, Gregor mentions that "the lack of all direct human speech for the past two months" has confused his mind. The lonely quality of Gregor's bachelor existence assumes ever more self-destructive features, of which he is fully aware.

Time being so related to movement, Gregor's increasing lack of direction and continuous crawling around in circles finally result in his total loss of a sense of time. When his mother and sister remove the furniture from his room in the second part of the story, he loses his "last guideline of direction." Paradoxically, "The Metamorphosis" is enacted outside the context of time, and because of this, time is always frightfully present. As Kafka put it in an aphorism, "It is only our concept of time which permits us to use the term 'The Last Judgment'; in reality, it is a permanent judgment."

Gregor is doomed without knowing the charges or the verdict, and all he can do is bow to a powerful Unknown. And this is all the reader can do. Following the narrator, he can view all angles of Gregor's torment. Not one person within the story can do that, Gregor included. They are all shut off from seeing any perspective other than their own. This is their curse. There is no textual evidence in the story which explicitly tells us the cause of Gregor's fate. But because we too suffer from the sense of aloneness that Gregor does and because Kafka calls on us to share Gregor's tribulations with him, we discover that his experiences are analogous to our own.

"THE JUDGMENT"
(DAS URTEIL)

There are two reasons why "The Judgment" is considered the most autobiographical of Kafka's stories. First, there are Kafka's own commentaries and entries in his diary. When he re-read the story, for instance, he noted that only *he* could penetrate to the core of the story which, much like a newborn child, "was covered with dirt and mucus as it came out of him"; he also commented in his diary that he wanted to write down all possible relationships within the story that were not clear to him when he originally wrote it. This is not surprising for a highly introverted writer like Kafka, but it does illustrate the enormous inner pressure under which he must have written "The Judgment." In this connection, it should also be remembered that he completed the story in one sitting, during a single night; he "carried his own weight on his back more than once that night," he said, commenting that one can really write only in this manner, "completely open spiritually and physically." Indeed, everything Kafka wrote before "The Judgment" seems unfinished by comparison.

Second, "The Judgment" is partly the result of Kafka's fateful meeting with Felice Bauer (later, his fiancée) in the home of his friend Max Brod, six weeks before the story's composition (see Life and Background). Georg Bendemann's judgment at the hand of his father is as inexorable as was that of Franz Kafka at the hand of Felice, who was to create a dilemma between his ideal of bachelorhood—to him, the necessary prerequisite for his writing—and that of a happy family life. Immediately after meeting Felice, he wrote that he was "doomed," and some time after finishing "The Judgment," he remarked that he was indirectly indebted to Felice for the story, but also that Georg dies because of Frieda. From then on, Kafka never really stopped incriminating himself because of his feeling that if he were married to Felice, he would betray his art.

The story's most paramount theme, that of Georg's bachelorhood, has its origin in Kafka's complex relationships with his fiancée and his father, but also in his perfectionist notions of what writing should be. More than once, Max Brod wrote that Kafka was steeped in a trance during the autumn of 1912. Kafka regarded art as "a form of prayer," wanted to have nothing to do with writing for aesthetic reasons, and continuously suffered from the realization that he could not ever close the gap between what he heard inside himself and what he actually wrote. It is the realization of his impotence in the face of an Absolute that accounts for his terse and fragmentary, yet immensely dynamic, style — which is more noticeable in "The Judgment" than in most of his other works. Leaving so much unsaid which, Kafka felt, eluded his grasp as a writer, this style excites the reader's imagination and consistently drives him to question and comment. Better than most of his stories, "The Judgment" reflects Kafka's haunted mind, which, taking perfection and intensity of experience as its goal, races through the plot.

Kafka's curse of being able to write only in seclusion is the seemy side of his devotion to writing as life's only reward. In this sense, Georg Bendemann, like other heroes of Kafka's stories, reflects the author's most basic personal problem — that of bachelorhood. Kafka attempted to escape the conflict by being as pure a writer as possible, and in order to accomplish this, he "embraced" bachelorhood. The result was that in his stories the bachelor became an archetype of absolute loneliness.

A random selection of entries in his diary demonstrates Kafka's indecision and anxiety with regard to Felice. In spite of several letters imploring her to forget him because he would only make her unhappy, he nevertheless kept up his correspondence with her. He wrote of his desire for complete solitude, and yet only two days later, he dreamed of "growth and sublimation of his existence through marriage." He devised a list of seven points for and against marriage, in which he assured himself that everything he had ever accomplished was the result of his bachelorhood. He hated everything not pertaining to literature; he also dreaded the mere thought of having to waste time on other people. Yet he yearned for "a modest measure of happiness" as a family man. One of his most tragic entries reads: "I love her as much as I can, but my love lies stifled beneath anxiety and self-incriminations." For five long years, until after his second engagement to Felice, he was caught in this dilemma. In the end, Kafka's bachelorhood exhausted itself in the repeated description of its own contradictions. The same is, of course, true of Georg Bendemann, who answers his fiancée's argument that he should never have become engaged at all, by saying: "Well, we are both to blame for that."

Kafka's explanation of the names of the story's couple also sheds light on the heavily autobiographical nature of "The Judgment." That Frieda Brandenfeld is Felice Bauer is rather obvious. Less obvious is that Georg and Bende have the same number of letters as do Franz and Kafka; also, the vowel *e* in Bende is repeated at precisely the same places as is the vowel *a* in Kafka. While the first half of Brandenfeld may stem from Kafka's association with Berlin, where Felice lived (Berlin is located in the county of Brandenburg), the second half of the name Brandenfeld has, according to Kafka, a deeper meaning for him: *Feld* (field) is a symbol of the sensuous, fertile married life which he could not realize for himself. In *The Trial*, by the way, Felice Bauer will appear thinly disguised as Fräulein Bürstner, also abbreviated F. B.

The opening scene, on Sunday morning, radiates Georg's contentment, which, as the story progresses, will give way to a mounting emotional instability. But now, at the "height of spring," everything is fine, and the bridge connects the monotonous city on his side of the river with the "tender green" of the hills on the other side. The bridge is still intact as the symbol of communication, which it will not be by the time he uses it to jump to his death. As is typical of the beginnings of Kafka's stories, the hero finds himself awakening from a dream, or at least in a dreamlike state.

The basis of the story's structure — Georg's musing about his friend and the letter he writes — takes up about a third of the story. The letter is striking in that the one item which made Georg sit down and write to his friend is mentioned only at the very end: his engagement. Before breaking the news to him, Georg writes about the marriages of uninteresting people merely to test his reaction. To his father, Georg confesses that he wrote to St. Petersburg only to prevent the possibility of his friend finding out about his engagement from somebody else. Even after Georg had made up his mind to tell his friend, he is careful not to describe Frieda in detail. All we hear is that she is well-to-do and that the absent friend will have a "genuine friend of the opposite sex" in her. The letter reveals more about Georg's reluctance than perhaps he wants to admit: his reluctance to describe life at home as it really is; his reluctance to follow through with his plan to make his friend come back ("How could one be sure that he would make a success of life at home?"); and his reluctance, above all, to view his engagement without any reservation and to write about it.

Frieda is the symbol of the sensual world and, in this sense, the representation of the "normal" life Kafka really desired but could not attain. Naturally she senses Georg's reluctance and ambiguity toward her and insists that the distant friend attend the wedding so that this bond of bachelorhood can be dissolved. In the light of this, Georg's assurance to his friend that he will get along beautifully with Frieda is wrong: she realizes the potential danger to their marriage, and he is equally aware of the temptation in the form of this bachelorhood relationship. Frieda gains control over Georg to the extent he loses contact with his friend, and after discussing his friend with her, Georg says to himself: "I can't cut myself to another pattern that might make a more suitable friend for him." She remains the stronger and he becomes attached to the life she represents.

Who, then, is this friend whose very existence is questioned by Georg's father at first? He is absent, nameless, single, lonely, and unsuccessful. The only thing positive we hear is that he obviously sympathizes with the uprisings in Russia so much that he wants to stay there despite the uncertain political situation. The combination of political and religious imagery in the scene at Kiev suggests Georg's idealistic view of his friend pursuing some cause and of Russia as the source of social salvation—or at least rejuvenation. During his last visit he already had a full beard resembling the kind Russian monks used to wear. (The turn of the century brought repeated uprisings in Russia, the worst one in 1905. It resulted in the relative freedom of the press and the right of free assembly. Soon after, however, Czar Nicholas II succeeded in suppressing open revolution and had several leaders—Lenin, Trotsky, and Stalin— deported to Siberia. For more about Kafka's political views, consult Understanding Kafka.)

Georg's treatment of his friend is slightly condescending in tone, especially the paragraph beginning with "What could one write to such a man?" It is also highly ambiguous. He condemns him, and yet he pities him; he considers persuading him to return, and yet is afraid of the responsibility connected with it. He keeps toying with the idea of letting his friend know about his flourishing business, and yet insists it would look peculiar if he did it now. Most significantly, it is only with great reluctancy and countless reservations that he finally decides to tell him about his engagement.

Perhaps the distant friend is best described in terms of what Georg lacks and vice versa. His friend's business once flourished but has gone downhill; Georg's business has boomed. The friend once tried to talk Georg into emigrating because success was promising "for precisely Georg's branch of trade"; Georg thought of persuading him to come back. His friend has almost no contacts in St. Petersburg and is "resigning himself to being a permanent bachelor"; Georg is engaged. The question remains unresolved as to what his business really is. It is not ordinary, not exactly geared to money-making, and it seems to require isolation. Is it perhaps Kafka's own "branch of trade" — writing?

When Georg sits down to write to his friend, it is as if he were writing to part of himself. It is as if this were Kafka's soliloquy, told to his writing-self, full of all the self-incriminations and tortures he went through during the time he wrote "The Judgment." Successful in business, willing to enter into marriage — yet shuddering at the mere thought of business and marriage — Georg represents the bourgeois element in Kafka, the part that would love to quit writing for good and become a family man. In this case, the distant friend is the "inner Kafka," escaping his father's world and trying to pursue his writing in solitude. He develops the "yellow skin" and the religious visions of self-imposed asceticism, not unlike the hero of "A Hunger Artist." Considered in this way, "The Judgment" is really a story about the unrelenting "inner Kafka," defending himself against Kafka, the human being with all his weaknesses, rooted in the sensuous world.

However, the friend is also more than Kafka's "inner self," more than his symbolic perfection and more than his watchful superego. The atmosphere with which Kafka surrounds him is deliberately metaphysical and mystical. Georg sees him "among the wreckage of his showcases," a failure, a victim, almost a martyr. Yet he does not forsake the country which has ruined him materially; he has saved his spiritual purity. If he died, this purity and idealism would also die. If Georg died, this would only be the end of the Bendemanns. The friend survives, comes to control and, eventually, condemn Georg in the person of his father.

The autobiographical significance of old Bendemann emerging as his son's judge is obvious. In most of Kafka's stories, though to varying degrees, an overpowering father figure plays a decisive role. Georg's father "kept him from developing any true activity of his own"; "My father is still a giant of a man"; "Georg shrank into a corner as far away as possible from his father"; these are a few of the clear allusions to Kafka's own father. Yet old Bendemann's authority dissolves and he collapses on his bed after driving his son out of the room. He is the despotic father figure, the executor of a quasi-divine will. This realization that the judgment of the father, as well as the self-execution of his son, are in no way evidence of a tragedy and are meaningful only within the context of this story is important. It is the best argument against the interpretation of "The Judgment" as an expressionist horror piece (1912 is usually listed as the beginning of the expressionist movement in anthologies).

Regardless of which view of old Bendemann one has, he is also a symbol of the enormous force behind Georg's life with which he cannot come to grips. Here, Kafka uses his childhood experiences to give us a parable of how everything we cannot handle in ourselves continues to grow, is projected into the outside world, gradually eludes our control, and eventually turns against us. In other words, the death sentence is the result of Georg's father fixation, the real cause of his overriding sense of guilt. It is not that Georg is innocent and does not deserve punishment for his inactivity; it is the exclusiveness with which he keeps staring at his father that draws him into the whirlpool of self-annihilation.

That Georg has a guilty conscience is evident. The way he dodges his father's inquiry about the friend by answering "You don't really look after yourself"; the way he has neglected his parents; the way he believes his father has lured him into a trap: all these are proof of his guilty conscience. One issue of the story lies in Georg's recognition that his father's words are essentially just and therefore unbearable. As a consequence, Georg accepts his sentence without complaining.

Old Bendemann is also the embodiment of absolute law to his son, and the many references to his negligent physical appearance point to Kafka's use of dirt as an aspect of legal authorities. (In *The Trial*, for instance, Joseph K. finds pornographic literature as he prowls through the office of the legal authorities.) Old Bendemann has the quality of a god of wrath who punishes Georg for his failure to live up to the ideal of his friend (the "inner self"), the ideal of art as a form of prayer, and bachelorhood as the means of attaining it. One advantage of stressing this quasi-divine aspect of old Bendemann is that his bewildering contradictions about the friend's existence lose their paradoxical quality and can simply be ascribed to his ineffability. The view of him as insane has the same effect. The trouble with this interpretation is that the only scene which might justify it, the scene in which the old man plays with the watch chain on Georg's breast, is not proof enough. To see Georg's suicide as the result of the decree of an insane mind would reduce "The Judgment" to an unnecessarily complex story; it would leave us with the view that contradictions and paradoxes are simply insane. Nothing could be further from the intention of Kafka, who once remarked that to understand something and to misunderstand the same thing do not necessarily exclude each other.

A more likely, though by no means wholly satisfactory, interpretation of the father's contradictions about the existence of the distant friend is that the friend gradually ceases to exist in Georg's mind after the latter has betrayed his ideals. As a result, his letters to St. Petersburg do not reach a real friend, but are mailed to what we may consider the relic of happy childhood days lingering in Georg's mind. In fact, the letter announcing his engagement—the height of betrayal in his friend's eyes—severs the last link between them. Does Georg not sense its fatefulness when he stares out the window after writing it? To the extent that Georg becomes unfaithful to his ideals, Georg's friend becomes old Bendemann's favorite. Triumphantly, the old man admits he has been in touch with the friend all along, and he grows from a weak man in his dotage to an overpowering authority for his son. Alone like Georg—he is a widower—the father becomes the friend's representative: not only is this term taken from the world of business in which old Bendemann has moved, but it also indicates the great importance of the friend in whose name he accuses and condemns his son. Georg, however, is unable to see this representation because he remains attached to the sensual, empirical world. Only for a split second does his father's enthusiasm for his friend dawn on him when "his words turned into deadly seriousness." Old Bendemann's assertion that the friend knows everything "a thousand times" better is an indication of his closeness to him, as well as a literal allusion to the friend's power.

The old man then, like the distant friend, is neither a human being nor a symbol, but he is both. He appears to be interested after Georg reveals to him that he has written to his friend, but more and more he takes on the quality of a last authority for Georg in a legal and moral sense. According to Kafka, what the old and the young Bendemann have in common is symbolized by the distant friend, from whom they emerge in opposition to each other.

Georg's condemnation has a psychological aspect to it which builds up throughout the story and reaches a climax with the accusation old Bendemann hurls at his son before sentencing him to death: "Till now you've known only about yourself!" Then there is the paradoxical pronouncement itself that Georg was "truly" a child but "more truly" a "devilish human being." Here we have two norms contrasted which cannot be reconciled on the empirical level. The juxtaposition of these two adverbs illustrates the futility of empirical logic in the face of the Absolute and its unfathomable judgment. This knowledge of absolute truth that Georg experiences as the highest commandment and as a binding decree, this realization that he has irretrievably lost his opportunity to live because he has betrayed his "inner self" – they drive him to suicide. He has roots in this life, and yet he has spent his days trying to shun responsibilities and to avoid clear-cut commitments. This is his guilt. Faced with death by drowning, he desperately seeks to recapture the Absolute he has forfeited. Reminiscent of "The Metamorphosis" and, especially, "A Hunger Artist," where longing for spiritual food is a paramount theme, the Absolute is symbolized here by the railings Georg grasps "as a starving man clutches food."

Georg's death by drowning may be seen as an attempt to return to the unity his mother used to hold the family and the distant friend together, as we conclude from the fact that the friend — purity, idealism — never returns after the death of Georg's mother. Her lingering presence is still powerful, however, and even old Bendemann admits it was she who gave him enough strength to establish rapport with the distant friend.

Whether or not the "unending steam of traffic" drowning out Georg's fall from the bridge also has sexual connotations is a minor point. (The German *verkehr* means both traffic and intercourse.) What counts is that traffic *is* a symbol for life here, if only in the sense of communication. In the form of a motor bus, life silences a suicide, illustrating that his death is of interest only to him. Taken literally or figuratively, life on any level remains inaccessible to Georg, who dies from alienation.

Beyond all autobiographical and psychological considerations, "The Judgment" deals with the complex interactions of good and evil. Representing the purity of his friend, old Bendemann condemns the power which has corrupted this purity in his son. However, even the execution of this condemnation seems to be a paradox because the suicide toward which the story builds becomes an execution. Here, as in the case of other contradictions in other stories, let us remember that, for Kafka, truth always reveals itself in paradoxes. This is why Georg, the victim, is also the executor of his judgment.

Probably the most serious paradox is the absolute incompatibility of Georg's guilt and his punishment. Particularly in view of his love for his parents, which is present throughout the story and is repeated in a prominent position at the end, the gravity of the sentence is incomprehensible. Nothing except Kafka's lifelong, deep-seated, and colossal fear of his unpredictable father can possibly account for its justification. It lifts the story's second half to the level of a surreal and therefore a rationally inexplicable nightmare. The incredibly terse and dense language stands in horrible contrast to the dominant themes of anxiety and doom in Georg's mad rush to his death.

"A HUNGER ARTIST"
(EIN HUNGERKÜNSTLER)

The first sentence of this story seems to leave no doubt about the story's realistic content: "During these last decades the interest in professional fasting has markedly diminished." First off, then, Kafka induces a consciousness of time by tempting the reader to inquire into the situation of hunger artists *before* the present decade. But the sober, pseudo-scientific language of this first sentence tends also to suppress the reader's awareness of the essential *oddness* of the profession of hunger artists. Thus we have only a vague sense of something unusual. The result of this tension between the quasi-historical investigation and the strangeness of its object is irony. Full of meaning, this irony is the bridge between the story's factual style of narration and its abstract content.

This differentiation between two levels of time also supports Kafka's main theme: alienation. It is here presented in terms of the continued confrontation of the hunger artist with his overseers and his audience. From the audience's "diminishing interest" in hunger artists, to its "absence of interest" at the end of the story, Kafka uncovers the mechanism that deepens this alienation. The more the story progresses, the clearer it becomes that this is a parable of the author's spiritual quest, as well as of his relationship with the insensitive world around him. Like all parables, it has a firm basis but is open to more than one interpretation. That it is told from the point of view not of the hero, but of an independent personage outside the plot, is not an argument against this statement. The point where the hero and the world outside his own lie anchored is the narrator's mind. Emotionally disengaged, the narrator's view is both ambiguous and absolute in its pronouncements. Is it Kafka, the teller of the story, viewing the fate of Kafka, the hunger artist?

There is no limit to the paradoxical situations the hunger artist is exposed to. He, whose nature it is to abstain from food, "the very thought of which gave him nausea," suffers from the superficiality and callousness of the overseers who suspect him of cheating and, worse yet, from the greed of the impresario who forces him to interrupt his fasting in order to eat. Most of all, he hates those overseers who want to give him the chance of refreshment, "which they believed he could obtain privately." He prefers being severely checked by the "butchers" among the overseers because, this way, he can prove his seriousness and integrity. These "butchers" belong to the realm of "raw chunks of meat" and the "stench of the menagerie," near which the cage with the artist is set up. They literally prove the validity of fasting to him, simply by existing. (A lifelong vegetarian, Kafka was, literally, the very opposite of a "butcher.") It is exactly through his starving that he tries to cope with them. He suffers in his cage, the symbol of his lack of freedom, but he prefers to starve for the eventual attainment of spiritual freedom rather than accept any of the pseudo-salvations of the realm of the "butchers" — that is, the world around him.

The overseers judge him by their own mediocrity and impotence and have no understanding of his professional code, which forbids him to swallow the least bit of food — were he ever to feel a need to do so (which is impossible in the context of this story). That his fasting may not be a virtue because it is the result of his nature rather than a self-sacrifice, is a different issue and certainly does not bother the overseers. As far as they are concerned, he remains virtuous (and insane which, in their value system, is the same) as long as he does not cheat, even though, as we have said, they do not expect him to live up to his vows. At times, the artist even takes to singing for as long as he can to show that he is not taking food secretly. The reaction of the overseers, however, is surprise at his skill to eat even while singing. Few passages in literature describe the fate of artists as solitary singers in the wilderness more dramatically. This is, of course, one of the tragedies of life: there is no way in which the morally superior can *prove* their truthfulness to anybody unwilling or unable to believe it. As Kafka puts it here: "The fasting was truly taxing and continuous. Only the artist himself could know that."

So wide is the gap of understanding between the hunger artist and the overseers that one of them will "tap his forehead" with his finger to signal that the artist is insane. The impresario, "his partner in an unparalleled career," actively exploits him. He arranges the hunger artist's life according to the whims of his audience and his own. When a spectator remarks that it is probably the lack of food that makes our hero look so melancholic, the impresario has nothing better to do but to apologize for the physical appearance of his performer, to praise his ambition and "self-denial," and to agree with the remark. This is too much for the artist to bear because it literally turns upside-down the cause and effect of his fasting. He is melancholic not because he does not eat, but because he is continuously tempted to abandon his fasting and to accept the very food he tries to evade. Sometimes he also reacts with outbursts of anger when the merits of his fasting are questioned or when a spectator tries to console him because he looks so thin. Here Kafka succeeds in driving to an extreme the paradox of the hunger artist subsisting on fasting. With it, he also achieves the purest form of irony.

The people — the overseers and the audience — have the feeling that something is wrong with the hunger artist. Being snared in the logic of their minds, however, they never see beyond one and the same suspicion: the artist must be cheating. This limitation of their vision keeps them from uncovering his real cheating — namely, that of making a virtue out of his "misery." "He alone knew what no other initiate knew: how easy it was to fast." This sentence is the key to understanding why the hunger artist is so dissatisfied with himself: he wants to live, and in the context of this paradoxical story the way to live is *not* to eat. His fasting is an art, though, and art requires to be acknowledged as achievement. It needs to be accepted as the ability to do something positive, whereas in the case of the hunger artist it turns out to be only a necessity, the surrogate for his inability to live on earthly food. Note especially his confession at the end of the story when he breaks down under the burden of his guilt. Ironically, he becomes fully aware of his guilt at precisely the instant when one of his overseers, moved by the sight of the dying artist, answers his confession ("I always wanted you to admire my fasting") by assuring him that he actually *has* admired him.

To Kafka, fasting is tantamount to being engaged in a spiritual battle against the enemies in this world. But to be thus engaged is his nature. In one of his fragments he says, "Others also fight, but I fight more than they. They fight like in a dream, but I stepped forward to fight consciously with all my might . . . why have I given up the multitude? Why am I target number one for the enemy? I don't know. Another life didn't seem to be worth living to me." And we might safely add, another life would not have been possible for him. In our story, the artist, barely able to utter his last words to the overseer, confesses that he, had he only found the food he liked, would have eaten it like anybody else. He does not transcend life by fasting, but he is fasting in order to survive. His fasting is not opposed to life; it merely makes it possible for him to bear it at all. If the hunger artist needs fasting to survive in the spiritual desert, Kafka needed his writing. In this sense, the story is a parable of the author's own lifelong spiritual quest.

Unlike the hunger artist, however, Kafka never thought of his art as a great achievement. The hunger artist does not merely exist and fast, but he also deliberately and consistently exhibits himself. His vanity leads him to ponder why he should be cheated of the fame he would get for breaking his own record by a "performance beyond human imagination." Kafka was the very opposite: he was overly harsh against himself when it came to judging his work. That his nature forced him to sacrifice his whole life, including three engagements, to writing—this fact he considered, above all, a curse. The hunger artist parades his fasting as a virtue, whereas Kafka was so convinced of the irrelevance of his art that he requested that his manuscripts be burned after his death. Or is Kafka's conviction perhaps only pride on a larger scale, the pride of an obsessed mind that takes absolute knowledge as its goal and suffers ever-new agonies because this knowledge is bound to remain fragmentary?

No doubt Kafka overstates the insensitivity and the lack of engagement of the overseers and the audience in the story. Yet we must not make the mistake of confusing his criticism with value judgment: nowhere does he consider the artist as superior because he is more "sensitive," and nowhere does he ridicule the audience or the overseers as despicable because they are callous, gullible, or even brutal. There is certainly more excitement connected with watching a panther than there is with staring at the solitary hunger artist. No doubt, also, panther-watchers are artistically less demanding and more likely to be fascinated by raw force. It was, nevertheless, *not* Kafka's intention to label panther-watching an inferior pastime. He, for one, suffered too much from the lack of the "panther" in himself to despise the animal. After all, the panther possesses, in a sense, freedom even though he is in a cage; his freedom is a freedom from consciousness — a state Kafka longed for. Too, the audience can hardly bear watching the "joy of life" and the "ardent passion" exuding from the beast. Kafka is simply pitting two equally justified forces against each other: the yearning for spiritual nourishment of the hunger artist against the elemental affirmation of life by the many. If Kafka condemns anybody, it is the hunger artist who should have pursued his vocation *away* from spectators and for its own sake. Not even the tremendous admiration of the audience for the hunger artist can, as long as it lasts, be said to be a success for him in Kafka's view because it is based on a serious misjudgment of the artist's intention.

Let us revert to the two opposing forces determining our lives, one pushing in the direction of spiritualization and beyond, the other one pulling back toward the animalistic sphere. In the interest of his own survival, man, according to Kafka, must not permit himself to be governed by either one of the two. If he did, he would find himself in a spiritual realm and thus become incapable of carrying on, or else he would relapse into a pre-human realm. In his diary, Kafka referred to these opposing forces as "the assault from above" and the one "from below." He explained his desire to escape from the world in terms of the "assault from above." All of Kafka's stories are permeated and deal with this opposition, but few show it as clearly as does "A Hunger Artist." The hero's loathing for regular food and his desire to fast to unprecedented perfection are the workings of this force and pull him from earthly life. The wild animals' and, especially, the panther's taking his place represent life-affirming forces. The audience moves between these two opposing forces, but it does not have the capability of either the hunger artist or the panther. Their fate is mere passivity.

The tight structure of the story neatly divides it into two parts, whose major difference may be discussed in terms of these two opposed forces. The first part reveals both forces at work within the hunger artist, the force driving him to fast and the elemental force sustaining his desire to survive. The drive to fast is stronger in the first part, and his art brings him success and even moments of enjoyment. In the second part—for all practical purposes beginning with the words "a few weeks later"—the artist fasts even though the audience stays away. The "assault from above" is gaining the upper hand and begins to mark him for destruction. Without an audience, he lacks the affirmation of his outward existence. As a result, the force counteracting his desire to fast is becoming increasingly weaker. This life-sustaining elemental force lies no longer within him but within the beasts next door. More and more, they are attracting the crowd, which now considers him only as an obstacle on their way to the stables. The crowd shifts their attention to whatever is most exciting at the moment and thus mills around the cage of the panther. That the artist's cage was placed so close to the animals "made it too easy for people to make their choice." At the end, when he has starved himself to death, the embodiment of sheer vitality appears as his principal enemy: the panther.

If we look at the two parts in terms of the relationship between the hunger artist's fasting and truth, we can say that the perversion of truth becomes greater the more his art is lowered to the level of show. The more successful his show is, the less true it is. Typically enough, the highpoint of his outward success, the fortieth day of fasting, beyond which he was not allowed to go by the impresario for commercial reasons, is also the point at which the hunger artist suffers defeat. As a "reward" for his fasting, he, whose sole desire it is to find spiritual food, is offered precisely the physical food he cannot eat. Here, as elsewhere in Kafka's works, the hero is tempted by women to abandon his goal: in "The Judgment," it is Frieda, in "A Country Doctor," it is Rosa, and in *The Trial*, it is Fräulein Bürstner and Leni. The impresario forces the food between the stubborn artist's lips while a military band drowns the scene in cheerful music and enthusiastic crowds swarm around the "flower-bedecked cage"; at the same time, the image of the circus, a frequent one in Kafka's works, reflects all the absurdities of this world. In the second part, when nobody cares for the hunger artist, he can live for his fasting. For his best performance, nobody forces a reward on him, and "no one, not even the hunger artist himself, knew what records he was already breaking." At his death, he is now at one with his nature and can finally ease his burden by confessing his lifelong guilt of having paraded his fasting as a virtue.

The sum total of truth (his art) and life are the same at all times, but one goes on at the expense of the other. By living, man gets in his own way as regards the fulfillment of his art, his search for truth. Expressed in terms of our story, it is true that *not* eating eventually takes the hunger artist's physical life, but from the debris of this life there flows forth a new, spiritualized life unknown to others. If the artist wants to find his truth, he must destroy himself. Suffering, here fasting, is the only possible way for man to redeem his true self. It is both the prerogative and curse of the hunger artist (and Kafka) that he is driven to follow this path to its inevitable conclusion.

The story of the man who lives on hunger contains the realization which Kafka consistently develops until the inherent paradox dissolves into two parts—the part of fasting and that of the elemental life force. Kafka may not make statements about something rational, but his paradoxes are highly rational statements.

"A COUNTRY DOCTOR"
(EIN LANDARZT)

Kafka used an unusual technique for telling his story of "A Country Doctor": he wrote in the first person, thereby imparting an exciting degree of immediacy to the story. The story is also exciting because of its fragmentary character—a symptom of

Kafka's searching mind, reflected here in an almost stammering rhythm. This effect is heightened by a lavish use of semicolons that chop up the already short and forceful sentences into even smaller units. An atmosphere of quasi-detached objectivity stands in almost eerie contrast to the story's dramatic impact and underlying miraculous character. Typical of Kafka, however, the language reflects the complete union between dream world and reality; in fact, the horses, ghostly embodiments of irrational forces, seem to drive, besides the doctor, even the author farther on. Kafka's recurring motif of the hunt (compare this story with "The Hunter Gracchus" and "The Burrow") has found expression in these galloping sentences, each seeming to chase the one before it.

The story begins in the past, switches to the present in the rape scene, reverts to the past, and finally shifts back to the present at the end, thus elevating the final catastrophe to the level of timelessness. At an even faster pace, images that share no logical connection with each other rush toward the story's last sentence: "A false alarm on the night bell once answered — it cannot be made good, not ever." Here is a good starting point for examining the story.

From the story's last sentence, it becomes evident that the whole story is the inevitable consequence of a single mistake. By following the call — a mere hallucination, a nightmare — the doctor triggers a long chain of disastrous events. His visit to the patient seems to be a visit into the bewildering depths of his own personality, for there is no actual ringing of the bell. The strange (and estranged) patient waiting for him does not really exist outside the doctor's imagination; he may be seen as part of the doctor's personality, playing a role comparable to that of the "distant friend" in "The Judgment" or the gigantic insect in "The Metamorphosis." "A fine wound is all I brought into the world," the patient complains, thereby suggesting that the doctor is his potential healer and belongs to him. During his entire journey, the doctor never leaves the vast regions of his unconscious, of which his patient is perhaps the darkest aspect.

In portraying this nightmare, Kafka has succeeded in portraying the situation of the man who wants to help but cannot. Kafka may well have seen himself and the whole profession of writers in the position of the country doctor: a man fighting against ignorance, selfishness and superstition, he remains exposed to "the frost of this most unhappy of ages." This is a diagnosis not only of a specific situation but also of the condition of our whole age. This is why the patient's question is not if the doctor will heal him or cure him, but if he will *save* him. "That's how the people act in my district; they always expect the impossible from the doctor," he says, explaining why he—or, on another plane, the writer—cannot be of any real help to the patient. He finds himself confronted with people whose consciousness is still attached to the realm of magic. They reveal this by stripping the doctor of his clothes and laying him in the bed alongside the patient. "The utterly simple" tune following this ritual reflects their primitivity, which would not hesitate to use the doctor as a scapegoat and kill him if his art should not work.

Although "In the Penal Colony," written two years earlier, is a better expression of Kafka's horror of World War I, there is much concern here for innocent scapegoats. The anxiety prevailing throughout this story also reflects Kafka's problems resulting from his second engagement to Felice Bauer and his deteriorating health. Shortly after his condition was diagnosed as tuberculosis, he wrote to Max Brod that he had predicted this disease himself and that his anticipation occurred in the wound of the sick boy in "A Country Doctor."

There are many more autobiographical elements, none of them "proving" anything in the strict sense of the word, but all of them shedding some additional light on the gloomy world of Kafka. The story is dedicated to his father, who ignored it completely. The misunderstanding between the physician and the patient is a reflection of the equally barren relationship between the old Kafka and the young Kafka. Knowing to what extremes Kafka tends to carry the art of name-giving, it is easy to see that the servant girl's name, Rose, is by no means accidental: "rose-red" is the color of the meticulously described wound, and the color *rose,* as well as the flower, is an age-old symbol of love in its manifold facets. There is no need to insist on one specific meaning of the word, if only because Kafka himself does not. The meaning is clear, considering that December 1917, the year after he wrote "A Country Doctor," brought Kafka's final separation from Felice, his "rose" in both senses of the word.

The groom represents Kafka's sometimes almost obsessive fear of a sexually superior rival. On this subject, he wrote that Felice did not stay alone and that someone else got close to her who did not have the problems which he, Kafka, had to face. In the story, the groom certainly gets to Rose easily, and if she says "no," she nevertheless runs into the house fully aware of her fate.

"If they misuse me for sacred reasons, I let that happen too," the doctor says. Yet his sacrifice would be senseless because it is beyond a physician's power to help an age spiritually out of kilter. It is out of kilter because, as everywhere in Kafka's work, people have lost their faith and have taken to living "outside the law," listening to the false prophets of unbridled technological progress and conformism. The boy does not trust the doctor, and his family displays the subservient and naïve behavior of the average patient. As the doctor puts it: "They have discarded their old beliefs; the minister sits at home, unraveling his vestments, one by one; but the doctor is supposed to be omnipotent." This is why the song of "O be joyful, all you patients—the doctor's laid in bed beside you!" is the "new but faulty song": the empirical and the transcendental realms are no longer one; the only way they meet is in the form of a clash leading to a "false alarm."

Only if we understand Kafka's notion of disease as resulting from seclusion can we begin to understand the country doctor. He is the subject and the object of his long quest or, expressed differently, the psychoanalyst of his own inner landscape (on another level, our whole secularized age) *and* the patient. And Kafka, though interested in Freud's teachings, regarded at least the therapeutical part of psychoanalysis as a hopeless error. According to Kafka, anxiety and concomitant alienation are the direct consequence of man's spiritual withering, and all psychoanalysis can possibly do is discover the myriad pieces of one's shattered universe.

Without his doing anything special, the doctor draws exactly the help he needs when he kicks the door of the pigsty. Like his whole trip, the sudden appearance of horses, groom, and gig bears the mark of the miraculous and the supernatural. Ever since Plato's *(Phaidros)* famous parable of the chariot being pulled by one white horse and one black horse, symbolizing the bright and the dark aspects of irrationality (rationality is in charge and tries to steer a middle course), horses have symbolized instincts and drives. The fact that they have come out of a pigsty here underscores their animalistic nature. Twice the doctor complains that his own horse died, and both times his remarks are accompanied by winter scenes, suggesting the barrenness of the (spiritual) wasteland around him.

Right away, the horses respond to the fiery "gee up" of the groom, who has already demonstrated his kinship with their world by calling them "brother" and "sister." The doctor also yells "gee up" at the end but, time being the correlative of experience, they will only crawl "slowly, like old men"; escaping from the patient and erring through the snowy wastes, the doctor has no experience by which to divide up time and, consequently, loses his orientation. The horses take over completely, at any rate, covering the distance to the patient's farm in an incredibly short period of time which, symbolically enough, is exactly the time it takes the groom to subdue Rose. Greatly adding to the story's dramatic impact, the doctor's night journey and Rose's rape are merged here on a logically inexplicable level.

"You never know what you're going to find in your house," Rose says, "and we both laughed." This line may be a clue. It is important that it is she who says this statement; she is better attuned to the realm of irrational forces than he, who spends most of his trip regretting that he has never noticed her, much less enjoyed her physically and spiritually. Now he realizes his negligence, but now it is too late because she has already been sacrificed to the groom. Her comment and their laughter at the sudden appearance of the horses reveal that these sensual and spiritual elements are present, but that they need to be brought out. On a literal level, this happens as they come out of the pigsty.

The closing picture of the fur coat trailing in the snow behind the doctor mirrors the helplessness of one who has been "betrayed." Traveling through endless wastes on his straying gig, the doctor is doomed to see the symbol of warmth and security without being able to reach it. Naked and cold and gone astray, the country doctor is the pitiful picture of disoriented mankind drifting over the treacherous landscape of its sick collective consciousness. And there is no end in sight because "he was used to that."

The question of the doctor's guilt provokes thoughts of uncertainty and ambiguity. As everywhere else in Kafka's work, the hero does not commit a crime or even a grave error. We are apt to get closer to the situation when we realize that he maneuvers himself, or permits himself to be maneuvered, into a state of mind which forces him to refrain from concrete decisions and commitments. In this sense, he becomes guilty of the classic existential sin—failing or refusing to become involved. By not taking his profession seriously and therefore lacking in responsibility, he forfeits his only chance of taking the decisive step from mere vegetating to conscious living. True, as a medical man he cannot be expected to save a patient whose sickness is, above all, of a spiritual nature. Yet he is guilty because he lacks the will to try his level best; he is afraid to act like a "world reformer" and pats himself on the shoulder for doing so much work for so little pay. Nor does he bother to view the wound as the result of the complex but undeniable interrelationship between physical and psychological factors of which Kafka himself was very much aware. Symptomatic of our age, the country doctor is the one-dimensional man who has lost a sense of participation, not only in the sphere of the sensual, but also in that of the spiritual.

Like the doctor himself, his "pack of patients" has stepped "outside the law" and into chaos. From there, they cannot help, the point being that they have lost the capability of doing that long ago. Whoever breaks out of Kafka's "human circle" alienates himself to the point of death. Kafka is most clear in this story: the impossibility of curing our age is his subject.

IN THE PENAL COLONY
(IN DER STRAFKOLONIE)

Schopenhauer and Dostoevsky are the two most likely spiritual mentors of this story. In his *Parerga und Paralipomena*, Schopenhauer suggested that it might be helpful to look at the world as a penal colony, and Dostoevsky, whom Kafka re-read in 1914, supplied Kafka with many punishment fantasies. It was especially Dostoevsky's preoccupation with the interaction between guilt, suffering, and redemption which fascinated Kafka. In this story, pain is a major precondition for comprehending one's sins: nobody can decipher the Designer's writing except he who has reached the halfway mark of his ordeal. Enlightenment "begins around the eyes. From there it radiates. A moment that might tempt one to get under the Harrow oneself." This is Kafka at his masochistic best. Yet there is also a philosophical meaning to this cult of pain. Insight and death go hand in hand, and transfiguration is the reward of those undergoing torture.

As for the punishment, or torture, however, even the simplicity and precision with which the remarkable "machine" operates cannot convince us that it is justifiable. Designed to imprint upon a condemned man's back the sin of which he is found guilty, it executes the sentence in the smoothest way possible. Everything is as simple as the "trial" preceding an execution, each cog fulfilling its proper function. But while the machine may enable the condemned person to "see" after the sixth hour, it does not offer him a chance to repent and to survive. He has neither the time nor the strength to do anything but continue suffering. Regardless of the gravity of his offense, capital punishment is the only possible verdict. As so often in Kafka's work, we are confronted with a punishment out of all proportion with the offense; in this case, the condemned man is supposed to fulfill the senseless duty of saluting in front of his captain's door every hour, thus missing the sleep he needs to serve as sentry during the day. The fundamental question is raised and remains unanswered: what logic does it take to condemn a man to death for a mere threat, particularly when he is described as a "stupid-looking creature"? At least, however, this story differs from "The Judgment," "The Metamorphosis," and "The Trial"; here, for instance, the source of the punishment and the charges are clear.

The torture machine is ever-present at the center of the story, the first sentence introducing it as "a remarkable piece of apparatus." Lifeless and fatal, the machine reduces the people around it to mere adjuncts who do not even have names of their own. Occupying an entire valley all by itself, it is a strange symbol, carrying out detailed instructions with utmost precision. It performs like the hand of some inexorable power, whose primitive nature is reflected in the stark landscape surrounding it and contrasted with civilization. In keeping with its commanding location, the machine is so high that the officer controlling it has to use a ladder to reach its upper parts. He who has helped construct the monster talks about its efficiency and intricacies with passion, yet it becomes clear that even this officer is the servant of his machine.

The secret of the machine lies in the mystery of the unusual order it sets up, sustains, and symbolizes. The nature of this order is so foreign to any conventional logic, including that of the New Commandant, that it must be assumed to serve a world beyond ours. The incident of the threatened captain is a good case in point: although he reports the incident to his superior, the latter takes it upon himself to sentence the man and put him in chains. He emphasizes that all this "was quite simple," proving that the machine and he belong to one and the same system, namely that of the Old Commandant, whose declared maxim was that "guilt is never to be doubted." This view reflects Kafka's conviction that man, merely by living with others and infringing upon their integrity, is bound to become guilty. Since nobody can claim innocence, it is senseless to collect evidence against an accused person. This argument is carried further in the scene in which the officer claims that to collect evidence against a condemned man would only cause confusion in his mind and that there is no need to explain the sentence; the condemned man will learn it best through his suffering. Unlike Georg in "The Judgment" or Joseph K. in *The Trial*, who both question the inhuman system persecuting them, however, the dull-witted condemned man in this story cannot do this.

The figure of the explorer is ambiguous. Hailing from Europe — that is, the civilized world beyond the sea surrounding the penal colony — he is on tour overseas to learn about foreign customs. Since he has been invited to attend this execution by the New Commandant, there is reason to assume he has been sent to pass judgment on this institution. Although as a guest he is determined to remain strictly neutral, he nevertheless has to admit to himself from the beginning that "the injustice of the procedure and the inhumanity of the execution were undeniable." Gradually, he becomes involved with the apparatus — for no other reason than that he alone is a foreigner and therefore *expected* to be neutral. He cannot be neutral; he condemns the institution of the apparatus, displaying the superiority of a man brought up in the spirit of democracy and liberalism.

The result of his condemnation of the apparatus is the collapse of the entire system on which the penal colony is based. Hurt and disappointed by the explorer's stand, the officer frees the prisoner with the ambiguous words "Then the time has come" and takes his place on the Bed of the apparatus himself. What happens is that the inhuman iron monster begins to collapse under the burden of the officer's self-sacrifice: "the machine was obviously going to pieces." What is more significant, the officer lying there with the big spike running through his forehead does not show the slightest trace of the transfiguration which every other dying man experienced under the grueling performance of the Harrow. This means that his self-sacrifice has been rejected by the forces controlling the machine. The words which he had the Designer write on his body, namely "Be Just," signify the end of that justice of which the officer has been the last defender.

It is difficult to imagine a more appropriate expression of the dehumanizing horror of World War I (at whose outbreak the story was written) than this symbol of self-destructive human ingenuity. Kafka succeeded beautifully with this machine; it combines all the brilliance of technological progress with the unspeakable primitivity of archaic, divine law.

The machine, of course, is also a symbol of the torture Kafka himself was exposed to as a writer. It is not exaggerated to compare the pain of creation with an execution; when he wrote, according to Kafka's own words, he experienced moments of transfiguration just like the condemned man here. Looking at the directions for the Designer, shown to him by the officer, the explorer cannot say much except that "all he could see was a labyrinth of lines crossing and recrossing each other, which covered the paper so thickly that it was difficult to discern the blank spaces between them." Prior to his self-execution, the officer shows the words designed to be imprinted on his own body to the explorer, who replies that he "can't make out these scripts." These are Kafka's allusions to his own writing — fascinating hieroglyphics and symbols of a horrible beauty that often bewildered even him. "Labyrinth" is certainly a most fitting name for the unknown regions through which Kafka's figures roam. All the explorer can do is admit that the writing is "very ingenious." What is self-evident and binding for the officer — that the inscription of the commandment violated by a man should be imprinted upon that man's body — remains unintelligible to the explorer, the outsider. This leads us to the story's other major theme, the officer's affiliation with the Old Commandant, whose "strength of conviction" he still shares.

The explorer is the product of a new system whose commandant, according to the officer, "shirks his duty" and is interested in such "trivial and ridiculous matters" as building harbors. He represents an enlightened and progressive system, which, however, does not meet Kafka's undivided acceptance as a meaningful alternative to the old system, as we shall see later.

The primitive order which the machine represents points to the dawn of civilization, which appears as a kind of Golden Age to the officer; he longs passionately for the restoration of a world dominated by a superhuman power. The outward perfection of the machine does not detract from its primitivity but heightens it through contrast, adding to it the dimension of the brutality of modern technology. Its destruction seems to stand as an indispensable prerequisite for any change toward a more rational and humanitarian system.

Change does not come easily, however, though the Old Commandant, uniting the functions of soldier, judge, mechanic, chemist and draughtsman, died some time ago (*Zeichner* is the German term for both "draughtsman" and "designer," thus indicating that the apparatus was, in effect, the Old Commandant's right hand). Though not the ruler of the colony, the officer carries on and defends the heritage of the Old Commandant against the new one. He is the "sole advocate" of the old method of execution, and he is thoroughly upset when the condemned man "befouls the machine like a pig-sty." As the embodiments of power in so many other Kafka stories recede from those who grope for an explanation of their irreversible fate—Klamm in *The Castle*, the legal authorities in *The Trial*, and the chief clerk in "The Metamorphosis"—so the New Commandant, like the old one before him, never appears on the scene personally. From the officer's fears, we gather that the New Commandant is a businessman rather than a supreme judge, that he does not care for the machine and the system it stands for, that he is eager to open the colony to international contacts and to grant it a hitherto unknown degree of liberal administration. In fact, the new regime is so open-minded that the officer takes it for granted that the visitor will be invited to participate in meetings on the future of the machine. Naturally, this strikes the officer as a further threat on the part of the New Commandant against traditional order.

As a result, the officer tries to coax the visitor into taking his side. In doing so, he talks himself into a frenzy, eventually assuming that the visitor has always approved of the old system anyway and only needs to choose the most appropriate language before the assembled administrators to tip the balance toward a revival of the old system. By trying to win the visitor over to his side, the officer clearly betrays the system he represents: without a single scruple, he sets the torture machine in motion whenever a condemned man was brought to him and never considered checking the evidence, much less exercising mercy. Yet he now asks for understanding and help. It is his downfall that the old system of absolute justice, which he represents, does not show human stirrings — even in his case. In keeping with its unbribable, clock-like mechanism, it condemns him to death. Now it is his turn to learn that, raised to the level of absoluteness, even such an ideal as justice becomes inhuman because it serves an abstract concept rather than human beings.

The officer's death, however, does not imply Kafka's wholehearted approval of the emerging new era. He keeps an ambivalent and ironical distance from the New Commandant and his reign. There is much change for the better on the island, as we have seen, but the "new, mild doctrine" has also brought with it much superficiality and degeneracy. Time and again, the officer complains about the great influence of ladies — even he himself "had tucked two fine ladies' handkerchiefs under the collar of his uniform"; these antics add a touch of the ludicrous to the new achievements. What Kafka is saying is that a certain measure of decadence seems to be inevitably a part of civilization and that the "modern" ideals of rationality and liberalism tend to give way too easily to considerations of utility and to the whims of the people.

To be sure, the explorer is interested in seeing the old system crumble. Yet he is extremely well-versed in abstaining from definite commitments, a trait which explains his reaction to the officer's description of the machine: "he already felt a dawning interest in the machine." Later on, when the apparatus is tried out, he completely forgets its deadly function and only complains that the noise of its wheels kept him from enjoying it all the more. When he finally realizes that the machine produces only horrendous results, he decides to make a compromise. Although opposing the system it serves, he is impressed by the officer's honest conviction. Not even when the latter places himself under the Harrow does the explorer lift a finger to stop the madness. Instead, he proclaims that he can "neither help nor hinder" the officer because "interference is always touchy."

The explorer shies away from committing himself because he has no binding standards. He expresses his disgust with the old system, but his humaneness is little more than a cover for his basic relativism. Especially at the end of the story, he reveals his true nature: already in the boat that is to take him to the steamer, he "lifted a heavy knotted rope from the floor boards, threatened the freed prisoner and the soldier guarding him with it and thus prevented them from leaping." His animosity is all the more surprising since he has played the decisive, though accidental, part in their liberation. It would therefore be only logical that he should show some concern for their future, should translate his theoretical condemnation of the old system into a concrete act of humaneness. By remaining unmoved, and therefore uncommitted, he displays cruelty which we may regard to be of a baser kind than the one shown by the Old Commandant, whom he condemned. Even the human element within the freed man does not really interest him. Reconsidering the story, we realize, as so often in Kafka's pieces, that the value judgment with which we may have identified ourselves in the course of our reading collapses under later evidence. In this case, evidence has accumulated that he who represents the "enlightened" ideals of tolerance and liberalism is not automatically superior to the Old Commandant and his admittedly outmoded and cruel system.

Kafka touches upon fundamental philosophical and political issues here. Ever since the time of the Greek political writer Polybius, human society has been confronted with the complex questions revolving around the apparently perennial alternation between tyranny and anarchy. From all evidence compiled over two thousand years, man, as a "political animal," has had to struggle to walk the thin tightrope between totalitarianism and the sometimes chaos which we have come to call democracy. Like a pendulum between two extremes, man's collective fate seems to swing back and forth between these two poles, symbolized in our story by the old and the new systems. On its way from one extreme to the other, the pendulum only briefly stays in the temperate zones — that is, democratic conditions are the result of a rather temporary constellation of forces. This is why the old system has had to give way to the new one, at least for the time being, but this is also why the Old Commandant will rise again when the new system will have worn itself out. Ultimately, neither system can last because neither can meet all of man's needs by itself.

On his way to the coastline, which is rather like an escape from the lingering spirit of the disintegrated machine, the explorer reaches the teahouse. It impresses him as being "a historic tradition of some kind." Upon his request, he is shown the grave of the Old Commandant, located under a stone plate. If there are indeed religious allusions in the story, they are most prominent here because the teahouse does resemble a holy place of some kind. The people gathered here are "humble creatures," wearing "full black beards" — Kafka's way of saying they are disciples of some quasi-religious mission. The inscription on the grave tells us that the Old Commandant's followers, now in the underground, will reconquer the colony after his resurrection and that they should be faithful and wait. Also, the explorer kneels down before the grave, and if he does so merely to be able to decipher the epitaph, he nevertheless goes through the motions of paying reverence in a religious manner.

Yet a total Christian interpretation is out of the question simply because the faith the old system rests on is one of sheer brutality. We have no reason whatever to assume that the predicted reconquering of the island will come about in a way other than through outright terror. This likelihood permits us to read the story, at least on one level, as a nightmarish vision of the annihilation camps of the Nazis. The story is religious only in the sense that the archaic system of the Old Commandant still prevails, though hardened into purely mechanical routine. Punishment by terror, which once meant purification and therefore was the focus of the colony's greatest festival, is considered nothing but a ridiculous remnant by the new regime. The machine still executes people (until it falls apart), but the motivation is gone and moral codes are imposed which lost their power when people lost faith in the divinity that once instituted them.

As in every one of Kafka's stories, a basic ambiguity remains, last but not least regarding Kafka's own feelings about it. While it is true that he condemned the old system for intellectual and humanitarian reasons, it is no less true that he lived with the uneasy awareness that the old system expresses a deep truth about human nature: suffering is part and parcel of man's nature, and the choice he has is not between accepting and rejecting it, but only between bestowing meaning to it or dragging it along as a stigma of the absurd.

THE HUNTER GRACCHUS
(DER JÄGER GRACCHUS)

Kafka's stories often deal with the power that either drives man beyond himself into the spiritual sphere or pulls him back into a primitive, this-worldly realm. (Compare the "assault from above" and the "assault from below" in "A Hunger Artist.") In several of his stories, he uses the symbol of the hunt to illustrate that wherever there is life there is also persecution and fighting. Nobody can escape it. A man may allow himself, it is true, to be driven in one direction by the hunt (as does the chief dog, for instance, in "Investigations of a Dog"), but having gone as far as he can, he will have to allow the hunt to drive him in the opposite direction and take him back if he wants to survive. Man remains the battleground of opposing forces, and this is why he roams the vague realms of life and death without being firmly anchored in either.

Few of Kafka's stories convey such a dense atmosphere of vagueness, remoteness, and dreamlike absurdity. This absurdity is intensified by the highly realistic description of Riva and the factual setting of the opening paragraphs, accenting a total lack of any common frame of reference between the townspeople of Riva and the newcomer. A touch of uncertainty and mysteriousness hovers over the story: the death ship glides into the harbor "as if" borne by "invisible means"; a man who is "probably dead" was "apparently" lying on a bier. Yet there can be no doubt about the "realness" of the story. To make this clear, Kafka has the hunter Gracchus remind us that, by contrast to the "real" world, "aboard ship, one is often victimized by stupid imaginations." In other words, the events taking place in Riva are not imagined by its inhabitants or by the hunter. In sober diction and short punctuated sentences, Kafka enumerates facts which, because of their almost meticulous factuality, stand in eerie contrast to the incredible occurrence itself.

Yet if the stranger's arrival is incredible, nobody really troubles about him or pays the least bit of attention to him. "Without any mark of surprise," the Burgomaster tells the visitor his name and profession, and the stranger's reply is equally calm. This contrast does not merely increase the impact of the story, but it also carries its own logic, in the sense that it reflects the impossibility of penetrating the story rationally.

It is of some interest that in a fragment belonging to the story, Kafka argues that Gracchus may be seen as an interpreter between earlier generations and those living today; he can transcend all limits of time and space ordinarily imposed upon a human being. Gracchus is capable of doing so because, as a dead person who is nevertheless "alive" in a certain sense, he has universal knowledge of everything that was and is. Comprised of both life and death during his travels in "earthly waters," Gracchus represents the totality of being, the universal elements of existence of all forms of being. This view is the only possible starting point for a logical explanation of how the hunter knows (or remembers) the Burgomaster's name. According to this explanation, the Burgomaster also participates in the timeless, universal quality of the hunter.

Who is the hunter Gracchus? Where is he coming from? We hear that he is "dead," and yet "in a certain sense" also alive. For hundreds of years he has sailed "earthly waters" ever since the day he fell into a ravine hunting chamois in the Black Forest. His barge was to take him to the realm of the dead, but it got off its course and has been aimlessly roaming the shadowy regions between life and death ever since.

While they know each other's names, the hunter and the Burgomaster know nothing of their respective worlds. Each is anxious to find out something but neither succeeds: the Burgomaster cannot even furnish the stranger with some desperately needed information about the town of Riva. This is, of course, a typical situation in a Kafka story: a complete lack of communication between people, or between worlds. The question arises: which world does the hunter represent? It is tempting to believe that the regions he comes from are a higher realm of reality, as opposed to the empirical world of Riva (which Kafka visited with his friend Brod in 1909). Once we analyze the hunter's world, however, it becomes clear that his world cannot be put into any fixed category. In fact, it is the most striking characteristic of the story of the hunter Gracchus that he no longer belongs anywhere, neither in a metaphysical realm nor in an empirical one. This was not always the case: he had been happy as a hunter, following his calling. He was happy even after he bled to death. Only long afterward did his mishap throw him into this predicament of total estrangement from any sense of belonging. We hear that it all began with a "wrong turn of the wheel" of his pilot and are immediately reminded of the "false alarm of the night bell once answered—it cannot be made good" again, the tragic insight of the country doctor doomed to roam through the snowy wastes.

Alienated and excluded from this world *and* the one beyond, the hunter Gracchus is at home everywhere and nowhere. Asked by the Burgomaster if he is not part of the "other world," he replies that he "is forever on the long staircase leading up to it." Typical of so many of Kafka's stories, this one begins with the hero's breaking away from a limited but clearly defined order. He once enjoyed living in this world, governed by a fixed set of rules, where people referred to him as "the great hunter." Now he who wanted nothing more than to live in the mountains must travel through all the lands of the earth and find no rest, even among the dead. All he knows is that no matter how hard he strives toward oblivion, he keeps regaining consciousness; he remains still "stranded forlornly in some earthly sea or other." The possibility of salvation does not exist, even under the best possible circumstances, because there is no way of communicating. Hence his frightening insight; to care is every bit as futile as not to care and "the thought of helping me is an illness."

As he so often does in his stories, Kafka drew on his own situation as a "hunter" here. The name Gracchus is derived from the Latin *graculus*, which means "raven," as does Kafka's name in Czech. Kafka repeatedly referred to himself as a "strange bird, aimlessly sailing about humans." Once upon a time it was possible to determine man's position in this world and the next one. As Gracchus puts it, commenting on his own death: "I can still recall happily stretching out on this pallet for the first time." Now he circles back and forth between spheres, and his apparently universal view of things is really that of Kafka, exploring all possible modes of thinking and living, dipping into each and staying with none.

As a result, the hunter Kafka was incapable of understanding the fixed order of earthly existence. He explained this failure in terms of a sudden lack of orientation, a distraction, "a wrong turn of the wheel." In his diary he referred to it as "self-forgetfulness," a lack of concentration, a "fatigue" which caused him to step out of the flow of time.

This lack of orientation and subsequent isolation, however, which permeates Gracchus' (Kafka's) life is not to be seen as something which one can explain autobiographically or psychoanalytically, as has too often been done in connection with Kafka's conflict with his father. The experience of such fundamental disorientation and isolation is rather the precondition for Kafka's uncompromising prodding into the complexities of human experience. That this human experience retreats even before his literary genius and permits only approximations is to be expected: language is by definition self-restrictive. What we term Gracchus' "totality of being" or his "transcendence of time and distance," for instance, we have therefore put in these terms simply because it defies any adequate description. This does not mean that "totality" and "transcendence" do not exist; the whole story illustrates that they do indeed exist. It is simply that to force Kafka's attempts to penetrate to the very core of the mystery of existence into a set of ready-made definitions would be tantamount to violating his intentions.

In this context, it is important to recall that Kafka himself has done everything, both in his stories and his commentaries on them, to qualify and even retract so-called clear-cut interpretations which he may have advanced or which others may have read into his writing. Naturally his stories are also interpretations and reflections, giving expression to manifold social, psychological, biographical, philosophical, and religious phenomena. But only up to a point. If interpreting were all he had had in mind, there would have been no need for him to leave his readers wondering about the answers to so many questions. The paradoxes and absurdities that abound in his works are the logical, because inevitable, expression of the fact that "reality" or "truth" on their highest level are indeed paradoxical and absurd when defined by our own limited comprehension.

THE BURROW
(DER BAU)

In terms of narrative method, Kafka writes from within the mind of the protagonist, and the introspective protagonist — through whose eyes we see the maze of the burrow — is the author himself. Any number of entries in his diary reveal the affinity of Kafka's existence with that of the animal, and in letters to his fiancée Milena, he even refers to himself as "the wood animal." But this animal is also man alone, man hunted and haunted, man confronted with powers that forever elude his control. And the burrow with its innermost sanctuary, the Castle Keep, is his painfully constructed bastion against the animosity of the world around him.

That the burrow's description so closely resembles that of an actual subterranean animal's hideout enhances its symbolic meaning and illustrates that it is really more complex than its outward appearance indicates. The "unique instrument" of the animal's forehead is a symbol of Kafka's (man's) passionate battle against the encroaching confusion of earthly existence, a battle he fought with "intense intellectual" rather than "physical" prowess. As he was to put it in his merciless, almost masochistic fashion: "I was glad when the blood came, for that was proof that the walls were beginning to harden. I richly paid for my Castle Keep."

What really is the burrow and against which inimical world is it intended? Let us view the animal's attempt to set up a shelter for itself in terms of a fight between mind and reality—that is, between man's effort to construct a rational world of his own making and the outside world dominated by irrational forces. It is against this incalculable world of irrational forces that he builds the burrow where he alone intends to be in charge. He believes his burrow will be superior to the reality of the outside because it is rational—which to him means perfect and entirely identical with its builder. (Compare this story with "A Hunger Artist" for another of Kafka's representations of the complete detachment of the outside world.) That his complete seclusion from the "real" world above results in an unhealthy preoccupation with it, is also the result of his failure to understand that everybody ultimately takes himself with him wherever he may flee to, thereby contaminating the imagined perfection of his new, artificial realm. For this reason, it is not exaggerated to call the burrow a solipsistic world.

The narrator's obsession with building a perfectly safe realm for himself dulls his mind to the decisive factor that, no matter how hard he tries to set up a self-sustaining world, this world will nevertheless depend on the outside for such basic necessities as air and food. The entrance, however, is not only the point of contact with the outside world supplying air and food: it is also the place where potential enemies can make their way inside. In other words, the impossibility of creating a perfect inner world goes hand in hand with the impossibility of shutting himself off completely. Hence the burrow will remain unsafe in the last analysis. The awareness of this imperfection drives him mad and, as a result, he will go on building and mending corridors as long as he lives. To live is to be afraid, and to be afraid is to be worried about defending oneself. The trouble is, as Kafka put it in one of his well-known aphorisms: "The hunting dogs are playing in the courtyard, but the hare will not escape them, no matter how fast it may be flying already through the woods."

The burrow is "another world" which affords new powers to him who descends into it from the world above. Time and again, it is praised as the sanctuary of tranquility and peace, sometimes even evoking associations of voluntary death. As in so many of Kafka's stories, the theme of hunting and being hunted figures prominently. In "The Hunter Gracchus," for example, this hunt makes the "wood animal" a battlefield of opposing forces — the "assault from above" and "the assault from below." Tranquility and the hunt, peace and annihilation — these are the opposite poles between which the narrator's life and our lives vascillate.

The entire story, it should be said, is dialectic in character. The burrow stands for the assumed safety of the animal's rational faculties, but it also stands for danger where "we will both blindly bare our claws and our teeth" when disaster strikes; the entrance symbolizes hope, but it is also the weak spot of his structure, through which the perils of the outside world threaten to leak in; and in spite of the owner's attempts at making himself independent of the outside world, he wants occasional contact with it because it exerts a certain fascination upon him. Outside "reality" even loses its horror for short periods of time for him, but he soon returns to his burrow, incapable of enjoying the freer mode of existence. Kafka has magnificently expressed the all-pervading law of movement and counter-movement here, a reflection of his own life embroiled in counter currents.

The description of the unknown and yet steadily approaching noise ranks among the most brilliant passages Kafka ever wrote. There are few pieces in which he caught the nightmare of his own anxiety-ridden existence in such fearfully dense diction. Comprising almost half of the story, beginning with his being awakened by an "inaudible whistling noise (the twilight zone of consciousness following sleep is most important in Kafka's stories), these passages are an ever-mounting frenzy of self-doubt, bottomless fear, and exhausted resignation. They seem to be one long scream, reflecting his own seismographic sensitivity to the tremendous, though partly still latent, upheavals of our age. At first, the builder of the burrow only talks about certain "small fry" that have dug their way into his domain, and what bothers him most at this point is that they have succeeded without his noticing them. Soon, however, the noise grows louder and keeps him on a steady alert. From everywhere within his burrow he can hear the whistling coming nearer and—this enervating thought completely overwhelms him—it may come "from some animal unknown to me." Battling his overwrought imagination, he begins to calm himself by imagining a swarm of harmless little animals. Once anxiety has made inroads into his badly shaken self, however, his agony is intensified. Reeling with visions of horror, he cannot keep the sound of the blood pounding through his veins distinct from the ubiquitous whistling any longer. Unable and even unwilling to trust his observations, he jumps to conclusions which he discards before he has even set out to carry them through. In a maddening escalation of frenzy, the invisible pursuers are holding ever more sway over him, alternately scaring him to death and lulling him into short respites of exhaustion. As everywhere in Kafka's world, it is precisely the elements of the unknown that cause his anxiety. (In fact, the psychological term anxiety (Angst in German) is generally used to describe feelings of being threatened that lack concrete, known reasons.) As sheer horror approaches, invisible and yet more and more audible, "the growing-louder is like a coming-nearer." Now he does not think of the source of his anxiety as a swarm of little animals any longer; it now begins to assume the looming proportions of "a single great beast." He goes into frantic last-minute attempts at fortifying his maze but, at the same time, he suffers from nagging self-incrimination because he has neglected to take defensive steps while there was still time. In fact, there had been plenty of time, for he was still young when he first heard the noise for the first time; as it happened, the danger subsided and, instead of taking this as a warning, he went on building his burrow as if nothing had happened. He begins to realize that rather than making him feel more secure, the burrow has weakened his ability to meet an assault successfully.

The most tragic realization in this story is that not even the best possible entrance or the best possible bulwark can save him, that "in all probability it would . . . rather betray" him. There is no direct correlation between the safety one desires, the efforts to achieve it that one goes through, and the realization of this safety. Or, expressed in terms of the story's main theme: in the face of advancing irrationality, man—relying on his rational powers—is doomed to failure. It is not enough to register the "scratching" of the enemy's claws, for whenever that happens "already you are lost." The irony is that there may be no objective threat at all, that the noise may be nothing but a projection of the dweller's own anxiety. He may have created a nightmare for himself, which of course does not make his agony any less harrowing. When we look at the story in this way, we realize that the whistling may well have been delusion, the result of his pathological preoccupation with himself.

On several occasions, Kafka referred to tuberculosis as being his "beast," and we may safely read the story on this level. Primarily, of course, it is a reflection of his own lifelong quest for security and salvation, as well as a sensitive diagnosis of an age which, while still deeming itself healthy and safe, was rapidly falling victim to the barbarities of twentieth-century political ideologies. "In the Penal Colony" comes to mind immediately, a nearly perfect portrayal of this "evil beast" at work. Quite in keeping with the intensity of its truthfulness to life, "The Burrow" has no end to indicate the termination of the drama described. Everything remains open and the battle rages on.

Whenever the hero of a Kafka story is also its narrator, we are faced with the question of who it is that he is actually telling the story to. To whom is it, for instance, that the dog in "Investigations of a Dog" tells about the research he has conducted all by himself and in which nobody else is interested? Or to whom is it

that the ape talks in "A Report to an Academy"? This is part of
Kafka's genius. The wide use of interior monologue designed to
record the internal emotional experience of the animal on several
levels of consciousness is most effective. Hence, also, the experience on the part of the reader as if the author did not exist, as if
he were overhearing the animal's articulations of thought and
feeling directly.

INVESTIGATIONS OF A DOG
(FORSCHUNGEN EINES HUNDES)

Like "The Burrow" and "Josephine the Singer," this story
deals with an animal that finds itself in a world beyond the empirical one. Unlike Gregor Samsa in "The Metamorphosis," the
animal is not abruptly torn out of a concrete situation and
plunged into a conflict with the universal sphere; instead, it is
encompassed by this sphere from the very outset. This immediate confrontation with the whole universe is a characteristic
of the later Kafka and may serve as an indication of his own increasing aloofness from "real life" concerns. He, the investigating dog of the story, is not "different from any other dog," and
yet he asks if it is possible for a creature to be "more unfortunate
still" than he is.

Looking back on his investigations, the old dog admits he
has always asked the most baffling questions rather than trying
to adjust to the ways of his fellow dogs. The result is that his
boundless thirst for knowledge has forced him out of his "social
circle." The event which set him on this path was his encounter
with seven dogs that turned out to be excellent musicians. Although that happened when he was young, he distinctly recalls
being overwhelmed by their performance in spite of his attempts
to keep his wits. Most significantly, the appearance of the seven
dogs was really his doing, at least indirectly, because he had
harbored a "vague desire" for such an event. It also follows from
the text that the light into which the seven dogs stepped was by
no means light in the empirical sense of the word. Both the
music they played and the dazzling light were really conjured up

by him whose "premonition of great things" had kept him blind and deaf. This explains why the music tears him away from his routine reflections and even robs him of his power of resistance.

The paradoxical nature of these remarkable dogs, the apparent "dumb senselessness of these creatures" which have "no relation whatever to the general life of the community," is an illustration of the inexplicable forces alive within man. Defying all clear-cut classification and behaving in a multitude of contradictory ways, these dogs are nevertheless most "real" in all their seemingly absurd "unrealness." As are the sciences of music and nutrition later on in the story, these beings — or imagined beings — are symbols of the futility of the dog's attempts at explaining empirically the reason of his existence. No wonder he thinks it possible that "the world was turned upside down." Again, the dilemma is Kafka's own: the insistence on the use of rational and empirical means beyond their legitimate range.

The music which the seven dogs play "appeared to come from all directions . . . blowing fanfares so close that they appeared far removed and almost inaudible." In his state of alienation, man is further removed from his innermost self than from anybody else. The ubiquitousness of this music seems to symbolize the totality of all things within which there are no barriers between the individual and the universal, between question and answer. Their refusal to answer any question strikes the chief dog to be "against the law"; in the sense that their music suspends the traditional order of things, this is correct. There can be no answer to any concrete question because this totality *is* the ultimate answer: the antithesis of question and answer, like every other one, recedes in one blaring sea of sound.

Kafka has attempted to describe this totality elsewhere. In *The Castle,* for instance, the protagonist K., as well as the people of the village where he performs his work, hears only indistinct murmuring over the telephone connecting them with the castle; this murmuring is said to sound as if it originated from countless individual voices merged into one single sound. Later on, K.

learns that this vague, drawn-out singing sound is all the people can rely on because all other "messages" are deceptive. It so happens that he learns this as he complains about the contradicting bits of information he gets from the castle officials. In other words, no single piece of information can amount to more than a fraction of the truth; also, our limited mind is necessarily partial and uncertain. In *The Trial*, Joseph K. does not understand the people talking to him in the courthouse; he merely hears a monotone noise permeating everything. It, too, remains open to a bewildering array of interpretations. "Truth," as Kafka put it, "lies in the chorus of the whole."

The annihilating quality of this music is, at the same time, the dog's safeguard for breaking out into freedom and toward a total view of things. His further investigations bear him out: at the end of the story, as he wants to die because he has not succeeded in leaving this "world of falsehood" for that of "truth," a strange hound appears to save him by chasing him away. He comes as a "hunter." (Compare this incident with "The Hunter Gracchus.") Exhausted and desperate, the chief dog does not understand and resists until he is again smitten by "irresistible" music. It threatens to destroy him, as did the music of the seven soaring dogs in his youth, but it enables him to "leave the place in splendid condition." As a puppy, he begged the seven dogs to "enlighten" him who "had roamed through darkness for a long time" and "yet knew almost nothing of the creativity of music." Now he detects a new life through the overpowering melody that "was moving toward only him." Now he has found "the law" of all creation in its application to himself. It is important to realize that it is only after his senses have been sharpened by fasting that he is rescued by the hound. "If it is attainable at all, the highest is attainable only through the greatest effort, and that among us is voluntary fasting."

The tragic realization remains, as it does elsewhere in Kafka, that this "law" and its liberating effect—here in the form of music—cannot be told." His speedy recovery and liberation is his own new reality. Even more tragic, however, this new state is also "delusive," not merely in the eyes of his fellow dogs, but also in his own mature judgment: "Certainly such freedom as is possible today is a wretched business."

The question of sustenance runs throughout the story until the investigating dog seeks to combine the science of music with that of nurture. When he asks himself if such a combination is possible, fully aware that he is moving in a "border region between sciences," he expresses Kafka's favorite theme of spiritual nourishment versus physical nourishment. In "The Metamorphosis," Gregor Samsa believes he has found his "unknown nourishment" in music, and the hunger artist sets his all-time record of fasting because he has not been able to find the right food to live on. Here, the dog has found out in earlier experiments that the earth does not merely supply all food by making it grow, but that it also calls down the food "from above." This is why he believes that not merely the indispensable task of working the soil is important, but also believes in "incantation, dance, and song," designed to attract food from "above." In other words, his concern is not with spiritual *or* physical food but with a synthesis of both.

This concern for the right food reflects Kafka's harsh criticism of traditional science as being preoccupied solely with working the soil. Though "to the best of my knowledge science ordains nothing else than this," the chief dog's investigations have shown time and again that "the people in all their ceremonies gaze upwards." Here Kafka criticizes both the scientific thinking that disregards the "upward gaze," as well as the quasi-religious stance which makes people "chant their incantations with their faces turned upwards . . . forgetting the ground." Despite his repeated professions to be a dog like all others, our chief dog differs from other members of his race in that his tremendous curiosity does not permit him to accept certain discrepancies. These pages show the dog (Kafka) pondering the fatal rupture between faith and reason (and between religion and science) that has run through our civilization since Descartes. To a large extent, the dog argues, a perverted science with a fixation on the measurable and statistical is to be blamed for the frightening success of so many pseudo-philosophies and surrogate religions in our time. By not taking into account man's need for food from "above," this notion of science has aided the confusion of minds.

Although the "theory of incantation by which food is called down" is a basic experience of all dogs, it is also an experience each one has to make himself. Therefore it eludes translation into the language of scientific proof. This is what Kafka means when he writes at the end of the story: "To me, the deeper cause of my lack of scientific abilities seems to be an instinct—and not at all a bad one. It is an instinct which has made me prize freedom higher than anything else—perhaps for a science superior than today's." Freedom is indeed the basis of the "science of man," even though its existence cannot be proven within the framework of conventional scientific methods. By deliberately risking his life, the investigating dog has shown that this freedom exists nevertheless.

A REPORT TO AN ACADEMY
(EIN BERICHT AN EINE AKADEMIE)

Wounded and captured by an expedition, a formerly "free" ape found himself aboard a boat headed for Europe. Confined in a tight cage, he realized for the first time that escape was impossible. Thus he decided to opt for something less than animal freedom—in fact, he didn't even require freedom. He simply wanted "a way out." For him, a "way out" required taking on as much as possible of the human world around him. This he did.

He succeeded in overcoming his animal existence to an astounding degree and, today, he is not really unhappy. Everything he learned he could not have achieved had he chosen to remain an ape, but: "One learns when one needs a way out." The seamy side of this statement is that the memories of his former life are becoming increasingly vaguer as the ape becomes adjusted to the world of man. As he takes on more characteristics of his human environment, he has trouble even comprehending the freedom of his past. It eludes his comprehension and even his power of description: the "direction" from where he came is really all he can tell his learned audience.

Yet, no matter how comfortable he may feel in the human world, the "gentle puff of air" tickling his heels reminds him, as it does every human being, of his lost freedom. (Cool breezes in Kafka's stories usually stand for freedom — sometimes too much freedom, causing man to lose his orientation.) The trouble is, however, that any regaining of this freedom could only come about at the expense of being a human being. To the narrator, the idea of being human and being free are mutually exclusive; maintaining a measure of each is therefore tantamount to being caught in the middle of two modes of existence.

This is exactly what has happened to him. He willingly shows his wound — this symbol of animal turned human — to visitors because "when the plain truth is in question, great minds discard the niceties of refinement." His development toward "humanness" is something he has aimed for, and yet it is a "forced career" he has never really wanted. His situation between two worlds is particularly tragic because he is actively involved in the human world during the day, in variety shows and lectures; by night, he sleeps with his half-trained chimpanzee mate. He cannot bear to see the chimpanzee by day, "because she has that insane look of the bewildered half-broken animal in her eye." He chose to turn human and has visible wounds and painful memories of a lost freedom, but she — still one hundred percent animal — is bound to go crazy among humans.

The narrator's position may be described as being between a past world in which he represented something he does not represent any more and a present world in which he represents something he *knows* he is not. This is why he begins his account with the words "I belong to the Gold Coast." His report deals almost solely with what he has experienced as a human being — which he is only in a more or less superficial way. His self-awareness was nonexistent when he was captured, and so he has to "depend on the evidence of others" when it comes to telling his audience about that part of his life. He apologizes for being in no position to supply any meaningful data on his former condition as an ape; his return to "apeishness" becomes more difficult proportionate to his development toward "humanness."

The language of this report bears the unmistakable marks of something artificially acquired. The enormous discrepancy between man and ape, as well as his attitude as an ape rather than that of a human being are quite evident, as, for example, when he casually boasts of having "emptied many a bottle of good red wine with the expedition leader" and when he jeers at such ridiculous human demonstrations of freedom as that acted out and applauded in the course of a circus trapeze act. Having achieved his goal to the degree which would guarantee his survival, he has learned how to participate in human society, even to be a great success in his performances. At the same time, it is important to realize that he remains a curiosity unable to bridge the gap between his two natures. Symbolic of his in-between situation, he thinks "with his belly." He belongs nowhere.

At no point in the ape's development in the direction of a human being is there any hint of a change for the superior. In fact, the story ends on a clear note of resignation that stands in sharp contrast to any belief in progress. There can be no advances without concomitant payments of freedom and life: "Even if my prowess and determination would be enough to get me back . . . I would have to peel every piece of skin from my body to squeeze through."

The story abounds in satire that sometimes borders on sarcasm, such as the description of the drunken ape accidentally gurgling "Hallo." The view is often held that Kafka permitted his ape to be raised to a level of "humanness" — a distorted one, to be sure — only to reveal the beast in man or, at least, the fact that man cannot attain his potential humanity in freedom. While not altogether wrong, this view does not do justice to Kafka, whose transformation stories are essentially parables of spiritual disorientation. In all of them, whether in "The Metamorphosis" or "Investigations of a Dog," the protagonist has not merely lost his sense of identity, but he has actually lost this identity itself. Whether the change is from man to animal or the other way around is beside the point: they all wind up in in-between situations. In all these instances, Kafka gives expression to this deepest of all human predicaments by using the essential "otherness" of man and animal.

THE GREAT WALL OF CHINA
(BEIM BAU DER CHINESISCHEN MAUER)

The discussion of the system employed in the construction of the wall takes up most of the story's first section. The way average workers react to the piecemeal system of building is contrasted with the way the sensitive workers react. This latter group would succumb to discouragement rather easily if they were to work far away from home, under difficult circumstances, without ever seeing their efforts come to fruition. It is only after they see finished sections of the wall that these sensitive workers go on performing with enthusiasm; being intellectuals and therefore more aware of the possible illusory nature of the whole project, they need continued reassurance of purposefulness. The piecemeal system was selected to give them this feeling of purposefulness (by having them marvel at finished sections) while permitting the high command to transfer the regular day laborers (who do not have this problem) to wherever they are needed. In its wisdom, the command has taken human nature of all kinds of workers into account by decreeing the piecemeal system.

In China, which Kafka uses as a symbol of the whole of mankind, people have been convinced of the meaningfulness of construction ever since architecture was raised to the level of the most important science. They are convinced because the workers have common plans and common goals. There is no chaos because no one is preoccupied with his own personal problems. The way for the individual to prevent chaos is by stepping out of his isolation, at least at certain intervals, and joining the great reservoir of mankind in a common ideal.

The narrator tells of a scholarly book which in the early days of the construction persuaded people to "join forces as far as possible for the accomplishment of a single aim." In those days, it was possible to achieve aims every bit as impressive as the building of the Tower of Babel although, "as regards divine approval," the Great Wall to be built is presented as a venture that, unlike the Tower of Babel, does bear the stamp of divine sanctioning. This book that the narrator cites says further that the Tower of Babel failed because its foundations were too weak, and that the "Great Wall alone would provide for the first time in the history of mankind a secure foundation for a new Tower of Babel."

The trouble is that the construction of a new skyscraper, be it ever so commendable an attempt on the part of mankind to fulfil its ancient dream of reaching the heavens, clearly goes beyond man's capabilities. This is why the new Tower of Babel remains something "nebulous." How can the wall be the foundation of this gigantic venture if it consists only of individual segments with numerous wide gaps not filled in? There is also justified doubt if the Great Wall will ever be finished. Kafka's comparison of the construction of the wall with that of the Tower of Babel has decidedly political overtones. In this connection, it is interesting to cite a passage from Dostoevsky's *Brothers Karamazov* (Part I, Chapter 5), with which Kafka was thoroughly familiar. There, in his criticism of political tyranny, Dostoevsky used the image of the Tower of Babel: "For Socialism is not only the labor question, or the question of the so-called fourth state, but above all an atheistic question, the question of the modern interpretation of atheism, the question of the Tower of Babel which is deliberately being erected without God, not for the sake of realizing heaven from earth, but for the sake of bringing heaven down to earth."

Fully aware though Kafka was of man's need for a common cause, he nevertheless shrank from endorsing any mass movement that enscribed the liquidation of the individual on its banners. His sensitivity to the emerging totalitarian ideologies of our century made him cautious and suspicious of "people with banners and scarfs waving." He detested and ridiculed their naïve belief in uncompromising solidarity for some version of perennial bliss on earth. His clear rejection of such ideologies is all the more remarkable because it demonstrates how well and consistently he could differentiate between totalitarian utopias on the one hand and the promise the Zionist dream held out to him on the other.

The greatest threat to which mankind is exposed comes from those fanatics who submit detailed blueprints for the wall and the new tower to be placed on top of it without having the right methods of construction. As the scholarly book explains, it is exactly this "nebulous" idea of a great common cause that appeals to people. Enthusiasm alone will not do, however. What makes the situation so much more difficult today is that almost everyone knows how to lay foundations well and the general yearning for a common cause has taken the form of yearning for *any* common cause. Naturally, the scholarly book is a great success with everyone now too: it gives people insight into their "essentially changeable, unstable" natures that "can endure no restraint" and will "tear everything to pieces" once it gets the chance to pool its energies. By revealing the counter forces to which people are exposed, Kafka has once again described his own situation — namely, that of a battle field. Two antagonistic forces are within him — the hunt that drives him beyond his limits and the forces chasing him back in the opposite direction, back to his concrete and earthbound existence. As he himself termed his anguish, he was continually torn by the "assault from above" and the "assault from below."

All we know about the nature of the command is that in its office, whose location remains unknown, "all human thoughts and desires were revolved, and counter to them all human aims and fulfilments. And through the window the reflected splendors of divine worlds fell on the hands of the leaders." These leaders represent the totality of human experience, and while they are far from divine themselves, they nevertheless reflect divine splendors. Like the officialdom in *The Trial* or in *The Castle*, the command may be seen as the symbol of man's spiritual world.

Remote, nebulous, and impersonal, it has probably existed from times immemorial. But it is also powerful and omniscient. And as in virtually all Kafka pieces, men rebel against an imperfect world created by a power which, they believe, could have done better. The human situation is aggravated because men have to assist in the expansion of this deficient world.

Any accusation leveled at the leadership is futile in the sense that we may say it is directed not at actual beings, but at man's world of imagination. This is why Kafka keeps warning us to try and comprehend things only up to a point. This message is clearly stated for us with the help of the parable of the river that floods the lands beyond its banks: as soon as man tries to transcend his limits — the "destiny" of the parable — he loses his direction. The thing to remember is that man's apparently innate temptation to attempt something beyond his limits is something the command has taken into account by ordering the piecemeal system of construction. As stated at the outset, the realization of the wall's imperfectability is something the workers could not cope with. Kafka has, of course, drawn his own lifelong battle here between his understanding "that the limits which my capacity for thought imposes upon me are narrow" and his unending, self-tormenting intellectual probing into the unanswerable questions of human existence.

Since work on the wall is completed (though large gaps will always remain) and since the narrator's "inquiry is purely historical," this probing continues. Doubt is expressed not merely as to the meaningfulness of the piecemeal system but also about the whole construction. Was the wall really intended to protect the land from northern nomads (Kafka's symbol of incalculable evil that might intrude anytime)? (Compare this with the threat of evil from the "outside world" of "The Burrow.") The mere mention of the nomads scares the children, it is true, but the enemies may very well be harmless fairy-tale creatures — again very much like the mysterious animal drilling away in "The Burrow." Surely the nomads are too far away to pose much of a threat. At any rate, the command's decision to have the wall built was *not* the result of this potential, if unlikely, threat because the decision is as old as the command itself. Man may mark certain points in time as beginnings and ends, but both the command and the building of the wall have been, and are, eternal. The decree to defend the territory against the nomads resulted from the wise realization of the command that men cannot survive without concrete tasks in a secured order of things or, to put it in Kafka's terms, "outside the law."

Empire is one of the most ambiguous institutions in China, as the narrator assures us at the beginning of the second part of the story in one of Kafka's characteristic efforts to dress the most profound questions in factual, quasi-scientific terms: the narrator knows a method whereby certain subjects may be "probed to the marrow" because he has studied the "comparative history of races." People do not even know the name of their ruler, and "Pekin itself is far stranger to the people in our village than the next world." Complete confusion prevails as to government guidelines and laws of everyday life, and any meaningful concept of time has been lost. As a result, dead emperors are venerated as if they were still alive and contemporary crimes are condoned because they are believed to have occurred in the distant past. Here Kafka has expressed a terrible insight about man, namely his tendency to turn his back on the problems of his own time and permit himself to be guided by the outmoded ways of thinking in bygone ages. Whole societies are fashioned after obsolete models, no matter how they terrorize people living now. The "law" of their own day remains hidden from them. This is their tragic fate.

The enormous distance between Pekin and the people of the south may also be seen as Kafka's illustration of Jewry outside history. It is a fact that Kafka chided Jews who deliberately forsook their own ways in order to try and become assimilated. If one reads the story on this level, China appears not only as the symbol of the universe but also as that of the Jews, scattered far from their spiritual center and yet, in a sense, held together by tradition.

If anyone should think that "in reality we have no Emperor because confusion abounds, he would not be far from the truth," the narrator says. Since the Emperor is immortal, however, at least as an institution, this means that man cannot know the institutions of the empire nor, as a result, abide by the laws it decrees. This is so not because the people have forsaken their Emperor: on the contrary, "there is hardly a more faithful people than ours." While one may read the story as dealing with the secularization of our age, the theme of the ambiguous relationship between the Emperor (God) and man is more paramount. Under no circumstances can the Emperor's message reach a specific individual because even the strongest and fastest messenger is bound to become lost in the infinite spaces between the imperial courts and the endless wastes beyond the palace gates. Only distorted fragments of a message may eventually trickle down to a subject, but even if this should happen, the message would arrive too late. Besides, the village people would not take any such messenger seriously and would probably kick him out anyway.

Nonetheless, the narrator says, we all "sit by our windows dreaming of such a messenger descending." A message would give direction and meaning. The situation resounds with all the melancholy of human longing for "law." The people, "insignificant shadows cringing in the most remote stretches before the imperial sun," stand no chance of making themselves heard at the distant court. It is partly beyond their capabilities to do so and partly due to circumstances they cannot change which keep them from succeeding. Yet subtly and consistently, an overtone of reproach is in motion which charges the people with not mustering up enough imagination and initiative when it comes to dealing with the cumbersome machinery of the state. As in the parable "Before the Law" in *The Trial,* where Joseph K. fails to act firmly on his own behalf against the clumsiness and callousness of a nebulous authority, Kafka attacks man's subservience before the state. The odds may be heavily against him and he may be aware of this, but he should nevertheless continue fighting. He must continue if he wants to secure a measure of dignity for himself in a basically hopeless and—which is worse—absurd situation.

This story is eminently "religious" in the broad sense of the term. Whether we interpret the empire to be a spiritual realm actually existing or whether we take it to be a figment of man's spiritually starved imagination, in both cases it serves to show human longing for meaningfulness. The empire's inaccessibility and the wall's imperfectability stand as convincing bits of evidence that man's desire and search for a fixed order must be thwarted unless he learns to employ the right means: it may be better, after all, to have old-fashioned believers than victims of "scientific investigations" into realms that must, of necessity, retreat before such probing. Kafka knows, as does the high command of the story, that people would lose the ground under their feet without some measure of hope anchored in the metaphysical. "Therefore I shall not continue probing these questions beyond this point."

JOSEPHINE THE SINGER, OR THE MOUSE FOLK (JOSEPHINE DIE SÄNGERIN)

The story's double title is one of its striking outward features. Kafka attached special meaning to this, arguing that it expresses an equilibrium, a set of scales, the careful weighing between the evaluation of Josephine and the people around her. While the meaning of "singer" becomes clear, however, Kafka's decision to use the term "mouse folk" is perhaps not so clear. Apart from underlining the aspect of mass behavior of the people who adore Josephine, he could have wanted to depict the miserable situation of Jews scattered all over the world and yet, at the same time, their sense of community as an ethnically and religiously distinct group. More than any other story of Kafka's, this one reflects his growing interest in, and defense of, traditional Jewish ways — above all, his positive view of the orthodox and Zionist sense of community.

The enormous power Josephine wields over the people is all the more surprising because they "forgot how to sing long ago" (they do not cherish their traditional Jewish ways any more) and do not care about music. Even more surprising, they agree that Josephine's singing is not really any better than their own. We are quickly told, however, that if this should be so, it is true only in a strictly musical sense; the essential difference between her singing and that of everybody else is still there: she sings consciously, whereas the people "pipe without thinking of it, indeed without noticing it." In her piping (for this seems to be all it is), the people's main characteristic — that is, piping — becomes a conscious action.

Another aspect to Josephine's singing leads to the people's identifying with her art. Not only does each individual listen to her singing as if he were listening for a message, but her singing "resembles people's precarious existence amidst the chaos of a hostile world." Totally absorbed by this tumult, they have forgotten about their true existence and have stopped singing, a reference to the secularized Jewry which Kafka came to despise. Whenever they listen to Josephine, the populace retrieves something of their short childhood, symbolizing a carefree (because less conscious) existence.

The narrator, the "we" of the story, tells us that nobody would really care to listen to a highly trained singer in times of general hardship; in other words, aesthetic perfection cannot be the objective of art in times such as theirs. As Kafka puts it here, "May Josephine be spared from recognizing that the mere fact of . . . listening to her is proof that she is no singer." People flock to her performances precisely because her singing is *not* art in the traditional sense of the word, because "it is not so much a performance of songs as an assembly of people."

Josephine, however, does not share the public's opinion of her singing. She is convinced that she creates perfect music, that her singing is infinitely superior to that of the people around her, and that nobody really understands her. She is certain the people are in need of her much more than she is in need of them. She insists that her singing takes the most decisive place in their lives and that she should therefore be exempted from all routine work. This alone would guarantee her ability to attain the highest possible artistic standard at all times. She desires nothing short of a whole-hearted recognition of her art as unparalleled and eternal. This is exactly the limit, though, to which people will not go. Such boundless recognition would be possible only if Josephine really stood "outside the law." If this were the case, the freedom from daily chores which people would grant her would be proof that "they are smitten by her art, feel themselves unworthy of it, try to assuage the pity she awakens in them by making sacrifices for her; to the same extent that her art is beyond their comprehension, they would also regard her personality and her desires to lie beyond their jurisdiction."

Here the essence of Kafka's view of art emerges — the view, that is, which he held toward the end of his life. He wrote "Josephine the Singer" in March 1924, three months before his death, and "A Hunger Artist," which also deals with the antithetical nature of art, two years before. In both stories, the protagonist falls victim to the temptation of deeming himself among the "select few," and in both stories his conflict results from his assumption that his art is vastly superior to the forms of expression of the people around him. In both stories, his refusal and inability to feel at ease in the "vast, warm bed of the community" cause his eventual isolation and death, and in both stories, his claim to stand "beyond the law" is rejected by Kafka. Even Josephine, whose magic makes people forget their hardships, has to remain bound by the laws of human community. The reason for this is that her individual self is at the same time the self of the people who find themselves reflected in her singing: whatever she may sing is also being sung by them, and whatever vision of freedom she may create is also present in the people sharing her performances. In its most profound sense, art is never beyond the people.

One may even go so far as to argue that Kafka foresees the disappearance of art in the traditional sense and, more important yet, that he does not shed a tear for its essential disappearance. "Josephine is a small episode in the eternal history of our people, and the people will overcome losing her" is only one sentence among many that reflects this view. The story is Kafka's final pronouncement on that esoteric notion that art is likely to die because it insists on being nothing but art. Everything seeking absolute perfection must necessarily refrain from becoming contaminated with life. But everything fleeing communion with life because of life's countless imperfections must die. To be perfect is to be dead. On one level, the story of Josephine is probably the story of a Yiddish singer-actress whom Kafka met in Prague in 1911, and on a higher level, it is the story of the universal artist faced with the large (mouselike) audience of our time. On still another level, it is the story of the inevitable death of self-imposed seclusion.

Historically speaking, the story stands as an attack on the obstinate arrogance of official art as taught and propagated by the academies of the nineteenth and early twentieth centuries. Rarely had art been more hypocritical, with its insistence on "higher values" and quasi-religious "purity." It is not that art cannot have these higher values and have this religious meaningfulness; it is just that in the nineteenth and early twentieth centuries, it had long lost the metaphysical basis for such lofty claims.

Josephine's last words stand as Kafka's own last words about his life. The mere fact that he prepared the story for publication from his deathbed, while requesting that all his other pieces be burned, attests to the significance he attached to it: "Josephine . . . will happily submerge herself in the numberless masks of our heroes and soon, since we are no historians, will ascend to the heights of redemption and fall victim to oblivion like all her brothers."

UNDERSTANDING KAFKA

A major problem confronting readers of Kafka's short stories is to find a way through the increasingly dense thicket of interpretations. Among the many approaches one encounters is that of the autobiographical approach. This interpretation claims that Kafka's works are little more than reflections of his lifelong tension between bachelorhood and marriage or, on another level, between his skepticism and his religious nature. While it is probably true that few writers have ever been moved to exclaim, "My writing was about you [his father]. In it, I merely poured out the sorrow I could not sigh out at your breast" [*Letter to His Father*], it is nevertheless dangerous to regard the anxieties permeating his work solely in these terms. Kafka's disenchantment with and eventual hatred of his father were a stimulus to write, but they neither explain the fascination of his writing nor tell us why he wrote at all.

The psychological or psychoanalytical approach to Kafka largely ignores the content of his works and uses the "findings" of the diagnosis as the master key to puzzling out Kafka's world. We know Kafka was familiar with the teachings of Sigmund Freud (he says so explicitly in his diary, after he finished writing "The Judgment" in 1912) and that he tried to express his problems through symbols in the Freudian sense. One may therefore read Kafka with Freud's teachings in mind. As soon as this becomes more than one among many aids to understanding, however, one is likely to read not Kafka, but a text on applied psychoanalysis or Freudian symbology. Freud himself often pointed out that the analysis of artistic values is not within the scope of the analytical methods he taught.

There is the sociological interpretation, according to which Kafka's work is but a mirror of the historical-sociological situation in which he lived. For the critic arguing this way, the question is not what Kafka really says but the reasons why he supposedly said it. What the sociological and the psychological interpretations have in common is the false assumption that the discovery of the social or psychological sources of the artist's experience invalidate the meaning expressed by his art.

Within the sociological type of interpretation, one of the most popular methods of criticism judges Kafka's art by whether or not it has contributed anything toward the progress of society. Following the Marxist-Leninist dictum that art must function as a tool toward the realization of the classless society, this kind of interpretation is prevalent not merely in Communist countries, but also among the New Left critics this side of the Iron and Bamboo Curtains. Marxist criticism of Kafka has shifted back and forth between outright condemnation of Kafka's failing to draw the consequences of his own victimization by the bourgeoisie and between acclamations stressing the pro-proletarian fighting quality of his heroes. That Kafka was the propagator of the working class as *the* revolutionary class has been maintained not only by official Communist criticism, but also by Western "progressives." And it is true that Kafka did compose a pamphlet lamenting the plight of workers. Yet in a conversation with his friend Janouch, he spoke highly of the Russian Revolution, and he expressed his fear that its religious overtones might lead to a type of modern crusade with a terrifying toll of lives. Surely a writer of Kafka's caliber can describe the terror of a slowly emerging totalitarian regime (Nazi Germany) without being a precursor of communism, as Communist criticism as often claimed. One can also read *The Trial* as the story of Joseph K.'s victimization by the Nazis (three of Kafka's sisters died in a concentration camp); it is indeed one of the greatest tributes one can pay to Kafka today that he succeeded in painting the then still latent horror of Nazism so convincingly. But one must not neglect or ignore the fact that Kafka was, above all, a poet; and to be a poet means to give artistic expression to the many levels and nuances of our kaleidoscopic human condition. To see Kafka as a social or political revolutionary because his country doctor, for instance, or the land surveyor of *The Castle* seeks to change his fate through voluntary involvement rather than outside pressure is tantamount to distorting Kafka's universal quality in order to fit him into an ideological framework.

Closely connected with the quasi-religious quality of Marxist interpretations of Kafka's stories are the countless philosophical and religious attempts at deciphering the make-up of his world. They range from sophisticated theological argumentation all the way to pure speculation. Although Kafka's religious nature is a subject complex and controversial enough to warrant separate mention, the critics arguing along these lines are also incapable, as are their sociological and psychological colleagues, of considering Kafka simply as an artist. What they all have in common is the belief that Kafka's "real meaning" lies beyond his parables and symbols, and can therefore be better expressed in ways he himself avoided for one reason or another. The presumptuousness of this particular approach lies in the belief that the artist depends on the philosopher for a translation of his ambiguous modes of expression into logical, abstract terms. All this is not to dispute Kafka's philosophical-religious cast of mind and his preoccupation with the ultimate questions of human existence. It is just that he lived, thought, and wrote in images and not in "coded" conceptual structures. Kafka himself thought of his stories merely as *points of crystallization* of his problems: Bendemann, Samsa, Gracchus, the hunger artist, the country doctor, Josef K., and K. of *The Castle* — all these men are close intellectual and artistic relatives of Kafka, yet it will not do to reduce his deliberately open-ended images to a collection of data.

Interpretations are always a touchy matter and, in Kafka's case, perhaps more so than in others. The reason for this is that his works are 1) essentially outcries against the inexplicable laws that govern our lives; 2) portrayals of the human drama running its course on several loosely interwoven levels, thus imparting a universal quality to his work; and 3) very much imbued with his high degree of sensitivity which responded differently to similar situations at different times. Particularly this last aspect suggests incohesion and paradox to the mind which insists on prodding Kafka's stories to their oftentimes irrational core. Kafka's pictures stand, as Max Brod never tired of pointing out, not merely for themselves but also for something beyond themselves.

These difficulties have prompted many a scholar to claim that Kafka rarely thought of anything specific in his stories. From this view, it is but a short step to the relativistic attitude that every interpretation of Kafka is as good as every other one. To this, one may reply that "to think of nothing specific" is by no means the same thing as "to think of many things at the same time." Kafka's art is, most of all, capable of doing the latter to perfection. Paradoxical though it may seem at first, viewing Kafka's work from a number of vantage points is not an invitation to total relativism, but a certain guarantee that one will be aware of the many levels of his work.

Despite the many differences in approaching Kafka's writings, all of them must finally deal with a rather hermetically sealed-off world. Whatever Kafka expresses is a reflection of his own complex self amidst a concrete social and political constellation, but it is a reflection broken and distorted by the sharp edges of his analytical mind. Thus the people whom his heroes meet and whom we see through their eyes are not "real" in a psychological sense, not "true" in an empirical sense, and are not "natural" in a biological sense. Their one distinctive mark is that of being something *created*. Kafka once remarked to his friend Janouch, "I did not draw men. I told a story. These are pictures, only pictures." That he succeeded in endowing them with enough plausibility to raise them to the level of living symbols and parables is the secret of his art.

Kafka's stories should not tempt us to analyze them along the lines of fantasy versus reality. An unchangeable and alienated world unfolds before us, a world governed by its own laws and developing its own logic. This world is our world and yet it is not. "Its pictures and symbols are taken from our world of phenomena, but they also appear to belong somewhere else. We sense that we encounter people we know and situations we have lived through in our own everyday lives, and yet these people and situations appear somehow estranged. They are real and physical, and yet they are also grotesque and abstract. They use a sober language devoid of luster in order to assure meaningful communication among each other, and yet they fail, passing one another like boats in an impenetrable fog. Yet even this fog, the realm of the surreal (super-real), has something convincing about it. We therefore have the exciting feeling that Kafka's people say things of preeminent significance but that it is, at the same time, impossible for us to comprehend.

Finally, the reader seems to be left with two choices of how to "read" Kafka. One is to see Kafka's world as full of parables and symbols, magnified and fantastically distorted (and therefore infinitely more real), a world confronting us with a dream vision of our own condition. The other choice is to forego any claim of even trying to understand his world and to expose oneself to its atmosphere of haunting anxiety, visionary bizarreness, and — occasionally — faint promises of hope.

KAFKA'S JEWISH INFLUENCE

Prague was steeped in the atmosphere of Jewish learning and writing until the social and political turmoil of the collapsing Austrian Empire put an end to its traditional character. The first Jews had come to Prague in the tenth century, and the earliest written document about what the city looked like was by a Jewish traveler. According to him, Prague was a cultural crossroads even then. Pulsating with life, the city produced many a lingering myth during the subsequent centuries, and they, in turn, added to its cultural fertility. The myth of the *golem* is probably its most well known: *golem* ("clay" in Hebrew) was the first chunk of inanimate matter that the famed Rabbi Loew, known for his learnedness as well as his alchemistic pursuits, supposedly awakened to actual life in the late sixteenth century. This myth fathered a whole genre of literature written in the haunting, semi-mystical atmosphere of Prague's Jewish ghetto. It is this background, medieval originally, but with several layers of subsequent cultural impulses superimposed on it, that pervades the world of Franz Kafka, supplying it with a very "real" setting of what is generally and misleadingly known as "Kafkaesque unrealness."

One of the unresolved tensions that is characteristic of Kafka's work occurs between his early (and growing) awareness of his Jewish heritage and the realization that modern Central European Jewry had become almost wholly assimilated. This tension remained alive in him quite apart from his situation as a prominent member of the Jewish-German intelligentsia of Prague. The problem concerned him all the more directly because his family clung to Jewish traditions only in a super-ficial way. Although perhaps of a more orthodox background than her husband—and therefore not quite so eager to attain total assimilation into gentile society—even Kafka's mother made no great effort to cherish Jewish ways. On one level, then, Kafka's animosity toward his father and his entire family may be ex-plained by his mounting interest in his Jewish heritage which they did not share.

Kafka felt drawn to Jews who had maintained their cultural identity, among them the leader of a Yiddish acting group from Poland. He attended their performances in 1911, organized eve-nings of reading Yiddish literature, and was drawn into fierce arguments about this subject with his father, who despised traveling actors, as did the Jewish establishment of Prague. It was at that time that Kafka began to study Hebrew. As late as 1921, however, he still complained about having no firm knowl-edge of Jewish history and religion.

What fascinated Kafka about the various members of this group was their firmness of faith and their resistance to being absorbed into the culture of their gentile environment. There are numerous letters and diary entries which point to Kafka's awareness of the essential difference between Western and East-ern Jews concerning this matter. Kafka felt a great affinity with the chassidic tradition (*chassidic* means "pious" in Hebrew; it was an old conservative movement within Judaism which came to flower again in the eighteenth century in eastern Europe). Kafka admired very much their ardent, this-worldly faith, their veneration of ancestry, and their cherishing of native customs. He developed a powerful contempt for Jewish artists who, in his estimation, too willingly succumbed to assimilation and secu-larization.

Kafka was particularly interested in Zionism, the movement founded by Theodor Herzl (*The Jewish State*, 1890) to terminate the dissemination of Jews all over the world by promoting their settlement in Palestine. Zionism preached the ancient Jewish belief that the Messiah would arrive with the re-establishment of the Jewish state, and Kafka's desire for such a Jewish state and his willingness to emigrate should be noted. Kafka published in a Zionist magazine, planned several trips to Palestine (which never materialized because of his deteriorating health), and was most enthusiastic about the solidarity, the sense of community, and the simplicity of the new *kibbuzim*.

While it is true that Kafka's friend Max Brod influenced him in supporting the ideals of Zionism, it is incorrect to say that without Brod's influence Kafka would never have developed an interest in the movement. His Hebrew teacher Thieberger, a friend and student of Martin Buber, was also a major influence on Kafka. Thieberger emphasized Jewish responsibility for the whole world and believed that everybody is witness to everybody else. Oddly enough, Kafka's father's steady exhortations to "lead an active life" may have added to his growing esteem for the Jewish pioneer ideal. Another source of Kafka's growing interest in Jewish tradition was, of course, his sickness, the very sickness that kept him from carrying out his plans to emigrate to Palestine and live there as a simple artisan. The more Kafka became aware of his approaching end, the more he delved into the study of his identity. A year before his death, he started attending the Berlin Academy of Jewish Studies, and it was during that same year, 1923, that he met Dora Dymant, who was of chassidic background and further accented his search and love for his Jewish roots.

It is clear that Kafka's interest and love for the various aspects of Jewry are not merely an attempt on his part to make up for past omissions in this matter. They are, above all, the result of his religious concerns — "religious" in the wider sense of the word — that is, religious by temperament, religious in the sense of ceaselessly searching and longing for grace.

KAFKA — A "RELIGIOUS" WRITER?

To know Kafka is to grapple with this problem: was Kafka primarily a "religious" writer? The answer seems to depend on the views one brings to the reading of his stories rather than on even the best analyses. Because so much of Kafka's world remains ultimately inaccessible to us, any such labeling will reveal more about the reader than about Kafka or his works. He himself would most likely have refused to be forced into any such either/or proposition.

Perhaps one of the keys to this question is Kafka's confession that, to him, "writing is a form of prayer." Everything we know about him suggests that he probably could not have chosen any other form of expressing himself but writing. Considering the tremendous sacrifices he made to his writing, it is only fair to say that he would have abandoned his art had he felt the need to get his ideas across in some philosophical or theological system. At the same time, one feels that what Kafka wanted to convey actually transcended literature and that, inside, art alone must have seemed shallow to him — or at least inadequate when measured against the gigantic task he set for himself — that is, inching his way toward at least approximations of the nature of truth. Each of Kafka's lines is charged with multiple meanings of allusions, daydreams, illusions and reflections — all indicating a realm whose "realness" we are convinced of, but whose nature Kafka could not quite grasp with his art. He remained tragically aware of this discrepancy throughout his life.

This does not contradict the opinion that Kafka was a "philosopher groping for a form rather than a novelist groping for a theme." "Philosopher" refers here to a temperament, a cast of mind, rather than to a man's systematic, abstract school of thought. Whatever one may think of Kafka's success or failure in explaining his world, there is no doubt that he always deals with the profoundest themes of man's fate. The irrational and the horrible are never introduced for the sake of literary effect; on the contrary, they are introduced to express a depth of reality. And if there is one hallmark of Kafka's prose, it is the complete lack of any contrived language or artificial structure.

Essentially, Kafka desired to "extinguish his self" by writing, as he himself put it. In terms of craftsmanship, this means that much of his writing is too unorganized, open-ended, and obscure. Even allowing for the fact that he was concerned with a realm into which only symbols and parables can shed some light (rather than, say, metaphors and similes which would have tied his stories to the more concrete and definitive), it is doubtful whether Kafka can be called an "accomplished writer" in the sense that Thomas Mann, for instance, can.

Kafka was, then, a major writer, but not a good "craftsman." And he was a major thinker and seer in the sense that he registered, reflected, and even warned against the sickness of a whole age when contemporaries with a less acute consciousness still felt secure.

The question of Kafka's being a religious writer has been going on for decades, but has often been meaningless because of the failure of critics or readers to explain what they mean by "religious." It is essential to differentiate between those who call Kafka and Kafka's works religious in the wider sense of the term — that is, religious by temperament or mentality — and those who assert that his stories reflect Kafka as a believer in the traditional Judaic-Christian sense of the word. Of this latter group, his lifelong friend and editor Max Brod was the first and probably most influential. A considerable number of critics and readers have followed Brod's "religious" interpretations — particularly, Edwin Muir, Kafka's principal English translator. However, for some time now, Kafka criticism has not investigated the "religious" aspect. This is so partly because the psychoanalytical approach and the sociological approach have been more popular and fashionable (especially in the United States), and also because critics and biographers have proven beyond doubt that Brod committed certain errors while editing and commenting on Kafka. While the original attitude toward Brod was one of absolute reverence (after all, he saw Kafka daily for over twenty years, listened to his friend's stories, and advised him on changes), the consensus of opinion has more recently been that, although we owe him a great deal as far as Kafka and his work are concerned, he was a poor researcher. He was simply too self-conscious about his close friendship with Kafka and therefore too subjective: he would never admit the obviously neurotic streak in Kafka's personality. While we may trust Brod when he claims that Kafka's aphorisms are much more optimistic and life-asserting than his fiction, it is difficult to consider Kafka primarily as a believer in the "indestructible core of the universe" or more pronouncedly Jewish-Christian tenets. His famous remark, striking the characteristic tone of self-pity, "Sometimes I feel I understand the Fall of Man better than anyone," is more to the point. We have no reason to doubt Brod's judgment about Kafka's personally charming, calm, and even humorous ways. It is that in Kafka's fiction, calmness is too often overshadowed by fear and anxiety, and the rare touches of humor are little more than convulsions of what in German is known as *Galgenhumor* ("gallows humor") — that is, the frantic giggle before one's execution.

In summary, one can argue in circles about Kafka's work being "religious," but one thing is clear: Kafka's stories inevitably concern the desperate attempts of people to do right. And as noted elsewhere, Kafka and his protagonists are identical to an amazing extent. This means that the main characters who try to do right but are continuously baffled, thwarted, and confused as to what it really means to do right are also Kafka himself. Viewed in this way, Kafka becomes a religious writer *par excellence:* he and his protagonists are classical examples of the man in whose value system the sense of duty and of responsibility and the inevitability of moral commandments have survived the particular and traditional code of a religious system — hence Kafka's yearning for a frame of reference which would impart meaning to his distinct sense of "shalt" and "shalt not." If one takes this all-permeating desire for salvation as the main criterion for Kafka's "religiousness" rather than the grace of faith which he never found, how could anyone *not* see Kafka as a major religious writer? "He was God-drunk," a critic wrote, "but in his intoxication his subtle and powerful intellect did not stop working."

KAFKA AND EXISTENTIALISM

Kafka's stories suggest meanings which are accessible only after several readings. If their endings, or lack of endings, seem to make sense at all, they will not do so immediately and not in unequivocal language. The reason for this is that the stories offer a wide variety of possible meanings without confirming any particular one of them. This, in turn, is the result of Kafka's view — which he shares with many twentieth-century writers — that his own self is a parcel of perennially interacting forces lacking a stable core; if he should attain an approximation of objectivity, this can come about only by describing the world in symbolic language and from a number of different vantage points. Thus a total view must inevitably remain inaccessible to him. Such a universe about which nothing can be said that cannot at the same time — and just as plausibly — be contradicted has a certain ironic quality about it — ironic in the sense that each possible viewpoint becomes relativized. Yet the overriding response one has is one of tragedy rather than irony as one watches Kafka's heroes trying to piece together the debris of their universe.

Kafka's world is essentially chaotic, and this is why it is impossible to derive a specific philosophical or religious code from it — even one acknowledging chaos and paradox as does much existential thought. Only the events themselves can reveal the basic absurdity of things. To reduce Kafka's symbols to their "real" meanings and to pigeonhole his world-view as some "ism" or other is to obscure his writing with just the kind of meaningless experience from which he liberated himself through his art.

Expressionism is one of the literary movements frequently mentioned in connection with Kafka, possibly because its vogue in literature coincided with Kafka's mature writing, between 1912 and his death in 1924. Of course, Kafka does have certain characteristics in common with expressionists, such as his criticism of the blindly scientific-technological world-view, for instance. However, if we consider what he thought of some of the leading expressionists of his day, he certainly cannot be associated with the movement: he repeatedly confessed that the works of the expressionists made him sad; of a series of illustrations by Kokoschka, one of the most distinguished representatives of the movement, Kafka said: "I don't understand. To me, it merely proves the painter's inner chaos." What he rejected in expressionism is the overstatement of feeling and the seeming lack of craftsmanship. While Kafka was perhaps not the great craftsman in the sense that Flaubert was, he admired this faculty in others. In terms of content, Kafka was highly skeptical and even inimical toward the expressionist demand for the "new man." This moralistic-didactic sledgehammer method repulsed him.

Kafka's relationship with existentialism is much more complex, mainly because the label "existentialist" by itself is rather meaningless. Dostoevsky, Nietzsche, and Kierkegaard all have a certain existentialist dimension in their writings, as do Camus, Sartre, Jaspers and Heidegger, with whose works the term existentialism has been more or less equated since World War II. These various people have rather little in common concerning their religious, philosophical, or political views, but they nevertheless share certain characteristic tenets present in Kafka.

Kafka certainly remained fascinated and overwhelmed by the major theme of all varieties of existentialist thinking, namely the difficulty of responsible commitment in the face of an absurd universe. Deprived of all metaphysical guidelines, a man is nevertheless obligated to act morally in a world where death renders everything meaningless. He alone must determine what constitutes a moral action although he can never foresee the consequences of his actions. As a result, he comes to regard his total freedom of choice as a curse. The guilt of existentialist heroes, as of Kafka's, lies in their failure to choose and to commit themselves in the face of too many possibilities — none of which appears more legitimate or worthwhile than any other one. Like Camus' Sisyphus, who is doomed to hauling a rock uphill only to watch it roll down the other side, they find themselves faced with the fate of trying to wring a measure of dignity for themselves in an absurd world. Unlike Sisyphus, however, Kafka's heroes remain drifters in the unlikely landscape they have helped create. Ulrich in Musil's *The Man Without Quality* and Mersault in Camus' *The Stranger* — these men are really contemporaries of Kafka's "heroes," drifters in a world devoid of metaphysical anchoring and suffering from the demons of absurdity and alienation. And in this sense, they are all modern-day relatives of that great hesitator Hamlet, the victim of his exaggerated consciousness and overly rigorous conscience.

The absurdity which Kafka portrays in his nightmarish stories was, to him, the quintessence of the whole human condition. The utter incompatibility of the "divine law" and the human law, and Kafka's inability to solve the discrepancy are the roots of the sense of estrangement from which his protagonists suffer. No matter how hard Kafka's heroes strive to come to terms with the universe, they are hopelessly caught, not only in a mechanism of their own contriving, but also in a network of accidents and incidents, the least of which may lead to the gravest consequences. Absurdity results in estrangement, and to the extent that Kafka deals with this basic calamity, he deals with an eminently existentialist theme.

Kafka's protagonists are lonely because they are caught midway between a notion of good and evil, whose scope they cannot determine and whose contradiction they cannot resolve. Deprived of any common reference and impaled upon their own limited vision of "the law," they cease to be heard, much less understood, by the world around them. They are isolated to the point where meaningful communication fails them. When the typical Kafka hero, confronted with a question as to his identity, cannot give a clear-cut answer, Kafka does more than indicate difficulties of verbal expression: he says that his hero stands between two worlds — between a vanished one to which he once belonged and between a present world to which he does not belong. This is consistent with Kafka's world, which consists not of clearly delineated opposites, but of an endless series of possibilities. These are never more than temporary expressions, never quite conveying what they really ought to convey—hence the temporary, fragmentary quality of Kafka's stories. In the sense that Kafka is aware of the limitations which language imposes upon him and tests the limits of literature, he is a "modern" writer. In the sense that he does not destroy the grammatical, syntactical, and semantic components of his texts, he remains traditional. Kafka has refrained from such destructive aspirations because he is interested in tracing the human reasoning process in great detail up to the point where it fails. He remains indebted to the empirical approach and is at his best when he depicts his protagonists desperately trying to comprehend the world by following the "normal" way.

Because they cannot make themselves heard, much less understood, Kafka's protagonists are involved in adventures which no one else knows about. The reader tends to have the feeling that he is privy to the protagonist's fate and, therefore, finds it rather easy to identify with him. Since there is usually nobody else within the story to whom the protagonist can communicate his fate, he tends to reflect on his own problems over and over again. This solipsistic quality Kafka shares with many an existential writer, although existentialist terminology has come to refer to it as "self-realization."

Kafka was thoroughly familiar with the writings of Kierkegaard and Dostoevsky, and it pays to ponder the similarities and differences between their respective views. The most obvious similarity between Kafka and Kierkegaard, their complex relationships with their respective fiancées and their failures to marry, also points up an essential difference between them. When Kafka talks of bachelorhood and a hermit's existence, he sees these as negative. Kierkegaard, on the other hand, was an enthusiastic bachelor who saw a divine commandment in his renunciation of women. For Kafka, bachelorhood was a symbol of alienation from communal happiness, and he thought of all individualism in this manner. This makes him a poor existentialist.

Unlike Kierkegaard, who mastered his anguish through a deliberate "leap into faith," leaving behind all intellectual speculation, Kafka and his heroes never succeed in conquering this basic anguish: Kafka remained bound by his powerful, probing intellect, trying to solve things rationally and empirically. Kafka does not conceive of the transcendental universe he seeks to describe in its paradoxical and noncommunicable terms; instead, he sets to describing it rationally and, therefore, inadequately. It is as if he were forced to explain something which he himself does not understand—nor is really supposed to understand. Kafka was not the type who could *will* the act of belief. Nor was he a man of flesh and bones who could venture the decisive step toward action and the "totality of experience," as did Camus, for instance, who fought in the French Underground against the Nazi terror. Kafka never really went beyond accepting this world in a way that remains outside of any specific religion. He tended to oppose Kierkegaard's transcendental mysticism, although it might be too harsh to argue that he gave up all faith in the "indestructible nature" of the universe, as he called it. Perhaps this is what Kafka means when he says, "One cannot say that we are lacking faith. The simple fact in itself that we live is inexhaustible in its value of faith."

In the case of Dostoevsky, the parallels with Kafka include merciless consciousness and the rigorous conscience issuing from it. Just as characters in Dostoevsky's works live in rooms anonymous and unadorned, for example, so the walls of the hunger artist's cage, the animal's maze, and Gregor Samsa's bedroom are nothing but the narrow, inexorable and perpetual prison walls of their respective consciences. The most tragic awakening in Kafka's stories is always that of consciousness and conscience. Kafka surpasses Dostoevsky in this respect because that which is represented as dramatic relation—between, say, Raskolnikov and Porfiry in *Crime and Punishment*— becomes the desperate monologue of a soul in Kafka's pieces.

Kafka's philosophical basis, then, is an open system: it is one of human experiences about the world and not so much the particular *Weltanschauung* of a thinker. Kafka's protagonists confront a secularized diety whose only visible aspects are mysterious and anonymous. Yet despite being continually faced with the essential absurdity of all their experiences, these men nevertheless do not cease trying to puzzle them out. To this end, Kafka uses his writing as a code of the transcendental, a language of the unknown. It is important to understand that this code is not an escape from reality, but the exact opposite — the instrument through which he seeks to comprehend the world in its totality — without ever being able to say to what extent he may have succeeded.

REVIEW QUESTIONS

1. What did Kafka try to express through the metamorphosis of Gregor Samsa?

2. Is Samsa partly to blame for having incurred his fate?

3. Samsa's metamorphosis goes hand in hand with a description of the world around him as he sees it in his new state. Give some specific illustrations of this.

4. The subject of the "earthly nourishment" and the "heavenly nourishment" plays a decisive role in several of Kafka's short stories. Which are the stories and how does Kafka deal with this subject in each of them?

5. In your view, does Kafka consider the hunger artist as one whose art is too advanced and too pure for the crude audience to appreciate, or does he finally call the hunger artist an arrogant show-off who does not have stamina enough to survive?

6. "A Country Doctor" has generally been said to contain the most clearly surreal elements of all of Kafka's stories. Do you agree with this view and, if so, what in specific would you say is typical of Kafka's surreal dream world?

7. In which sense is "A Country Doctor" the analysis of the spiritual disease of our age?

8. Explain why "The Judgment" is commonly regarded as the clearest reflection of Kafka's complex relationship with his father.

9. Discuss the differences between the reigns of the Old Commandant and the New Commandant in "The Penal Colony."

10. What do the two commandants symbolize in a religious and/or political sense? Do you have the impression that Kafka favors one of the two against the other and, if so, how would you support your viewpoint?

11. What are the chief elements of "The Hunter Gracchus" that make this story such a perfect parable of human alienation as it results from the loss of orientation?

12. Discuss the idea behind the "piecemeal technique" of construction as employed by the workers on the great wall of China.

13. What are the political ideas of "The Great Wall of China"?

14. Discuss the fate of the ape and his mate in "A Report to an Academy" in terms of his relative success and contentment versus her failure to achieve these.

15. What is the central theme of "Josephine the Singer"? Compare it to the same theme in "A Hunger Artist."

16. Explain why symbols and parables are better suited to deal with Kafka's main themes than are metaphors and similes.

17. What are the traits in Kafka's thinking that one could label "existentialist"?

18. Why is it irrelevant and meaningless to approach Kafka's writings with the attitude of explaining them rationally?

19. Why is the use of the term "Kafkaesque" dangerous for a serious and meaningful appraisal of Kafka?

20. Discuss whether or not Kafka may be called a religious writer.

SELECTED BIBLIOGRAPHY

BROD, MAX. *Über Franz Kafka*. Frankfurt, Heidelberg: Fischer, 1966. This volume was the first to contain Brod's three important pieces on Kafka. For over twenty years Brod saw his friend daily and discussed his work with him. Because of Brod, four-fifths of Kafka's work was not burned, as Kafka had requested it to be.

EMRICH, WILHELM. *Franz Kafka*. Frankfurt: Athenaeum Verlag, 1958. Dealing with a cross section of Kafka's work, the author argues that an autonomous logic prevails in Kafka's world of images. The book, which even Politzer lists as having most influenced his own *Parable and Paradox*, is permeated by an atmosphere of intimate contact with Western philosophical-religious tradition. The excellent bibliography warrants mention.

FLORES, ANGEL, ed. *The Kafka Problem*. New York: New Directions, 1946. A collection of essays on various philosophical, literary, and biographical aspects. Themes of special interest for a further study of Kafka are given preference over interpretations of individual pieces, although the two main novels figure prominently.

FLORES, ANGEL, and SWANDER, HOMER, eds. *Franz Kafka Today*. Madison: University of Wisconsin Press, 1958. The three parts deal with specific stories, the novels, and diaries and letters, respectively. Of special value is a complete bibliography of all of Kafka's works that have appeared in English and a complete bibliography of secondary material.

GRAY, RONALD, ed. *Kafka: A Collection of Critical Essays.* Englewood Cliffs, New Jersey: Prentice-Hall, 1962. The volume contains fourteen critical and interpretive essays from a wide variety of writers and critics. It attempts to do justice to the reading of Kafka by presenting his work from many different viewpoints, some of them strongly disagreeing with most Kafka criticism.

HELLER, ERICH. *The Disinherited Mind.* Cambridge, England: Bowes and Bowes, 1952. The tenor of the essay "The World of Franz Kafka" (the other two deal with other aspects of modern literature) is that Kafka, although fully aware of his own sickness and the sickness of the age, could at no point even begin to extricate himself from his personal tragedies. He would not and could not venture the "leap into faith" and can under no circumstances be called a believer.

JANOUCH, GUSTAV. *Gesprache mit Kafka* (Conversations with Kafka). Frankfurt: Fischer, 1951. Janouch, who met Kafka in 1920, participated in several translations of Kafka's work into Czech. The volume is a collection of letters, notes, diary entries, and personal memories. The material is therefore rather personal in character, expressing Kafka's views in the form of parables, aphorisms, and anecdotes.

KAFKA, FRANZ. *Letter to His Father.* New York: Schocken, 1966.

————. *Selected Short Stories.* New York: Modern Library, 1952.

POLITZER, HEINZ. *Franz Kafka: Parable and Paradox.* Cornell University Press, 1962. Politzer's Austrian-Jewish background and his friendship with Kafka were largely responsible for his undertaking the task, together with Brod, of editing Kafka's *Collected Works.* Foremost in this volume, which was started in the early thirties as his thesis, is the concern with Kafka's work as a literary document. The emphasis is on the three novel fragments.

REIMANN, PAUL, ed. *Franz Kafka aus Prager Sicht.* (Franz Kafka Viewed from Prague) Prague: Voltaire, 1966. This collection of lectures delivered at the now famous Kafka Symposium of 1963 marked a turning point in the Communist appraisal of Kafka. For the first time, the relevance of his work was admitted for Socialist countries as well. In the meantime, this cautious new approach has been completely reversed, especially since the Warsaw Pact Invasion of August, 1968. Once more, Kafka's work is regarded as decadent and irrelevant for Socialist societies. Since all contributions are by noted Communist critics and politicians — many of whom emigrated to the West after Dubcek's fall — the emphasis is on such concepts as realism, alienation, and the function of art in a Socialist society.

WAGENBACH, KLAUS. *Franz Kafka in Selbstzeugnissen und Bilddokumenten.* (Franz Kafka: Testimonials and Picture Documents of Himself) Reinbek bei Hamburg: Rowohlt, 1964. Largely biographical, this study shows the diverse personal, political, and literary influences shaping and changing Kafka's views.

NOTES

NOTES

NOTES

NOTES

NOTES

NOTES